TAKE 1

One Couple's Journey to Quit Their Jobs and Hit the Open Road

* * * * *

By Joe Russo
We're the Russos

Dedication

To Dad.
Your advice changed our lives.

FOREWORD
By Kevin Tumlinson

This is the book I wish I'd read two years ago.

That was around the time my wife (Kara) and I had a brief but interesting conversation while she stood in the doorway of my home office. "I think we should sell the house and get an RV, and travel full time while you write and publish."

Aside from the Scooby Doo-like noise I made, I couldn't answer "yes" fast enough! And at that moment, the whole thing started—a year of prepping the house for sale, picking out and buying an RV, and making ourselves ready for life on the road. And in that time, I did a lot of research, particularly diving into podcasts and vlogs, looking for people who were doing what we planned to do. That's how I came across 'We're the Russos,' and from there I had the honor and privilege of interviewing them on my show, the Wordslinger Podcast.

But I don't think I asked enough questions.

As it turns out, Kara and I had an experience nearly parallel to what Joe and Kait went through. We had triumphs and pitfalls. We had successes and mistakes. Never regrets, but a few miss-steps. In particular, we discovered halfway through our own journey that we had chosen the wrong kind of RV for the life we wanted. Cue more Scooby Doo-like noises.

All of that could have been avoided, had I just read this book beforehand.

This isn't a how-to guide. It's more of a how-we-did-it guide. From page one, you get to follow along with Joe and Kait as they make their decision, as they contemplate leaving their jobs, as they search for the perfect RV, as they, ultimately, take risks, and then reap the rewards.

That's the key theme at play here, by the way: Take risks. It's more than just the title, it's a decision, a choice. Joe and Kait decided that it was better to take a risk than to stay in the same safe, comfortable, but ultimately soul-numbing lifestyle they were accustomed to.

There's an apocryphal adage about insanity that makes its rounds on the internet: Insanity is doing the same thing, again and again, expecting a new result each time.

By that measure, choosing to risk everything and try a whole new life on for size has to be the very measure of actual sanity. Where some would look at Joe and Kait and wonder at their 'crazy' choice, they look at the world around them and wonder why everyone is so content to stay in the loony bin.

Again, I wish I had read this two years ago.

The popularity of RV life is growing at a rapid pace. Every day, people are embracing a full-time lifestyle of minimalism and expansive freedom. Maybe it's a sign of some cultural shift—a reversion to the glories of a nomadic life. Or maybe it's a sign of evolution, the opening of an inner awareness that yearns to see what's on the other side of that hill, what lays in that distant valley, who might be waiting on that other coast.

Whatever drives us to want to downsize, pack up, and get on the road, there are a lot of lessons we can take with us, expressed in the pages of this book. It's endearing, and sometimes alarming, but it is raw experience that brings with it a wisdom we all need. If you're thinking of starting your own RV life, your journey really does need to start here.

Kevin Tumlinson

Author, Host of the Wordslinger Podcast

July 12, 2017

PROLOGUE

"Take risks and have lots of children."

This is one of the last things my father told me before he passed away in 2013. By then, Kait and I had been together for eight years and our idea of taking a risk entailed not checking our work emails at night. Little did I realize that my father's words would be the driving force behind us quitting our jobs, selling our house and most of our possessions, and living a nomadic life wandering the United States in a motorhome. This story is about how we gave the modern definition of success the finger and took the biggest risk of our lives. This is our journey to living free.

1. MOTHER'S DAY

Saturday, May 10th, 2014

It's almost 7 a.m. and I'm lying in bed half awake. I've become so accustomed to waking up early every morning that I haven't slept in for years. Kait on the other hand is still sound asleep and apparently Leo, our white Husky (at least we think he's a Husky) is also passed out because I can hear him snoring. Heck, he could be part timber wolf for all we know, but that's the thing with a shelter dog, you never quite know. Duke, our Belgium Malinois, typically sleeps on Kait's side of the bed because it's closest to the door. He's 80 pounds of lean mean fighting machine and I sleep soundly knowing he's there. On the rare occasion I have to fly out of town for business, I know Kait is safe with Duke protecting the house and the family. Duke is also a rescue and when we found him, he was twenty pounds underweight and scheduled to be put down by the shelter. He's graying quite a bit and our guess is that he's about 12 years old but still full of life and acts like an adolescent most days.

Somehow with those giant ears of his he knows I am awake and walks over to my side of the bed, stepping over Leo so he can rest his head next to mine.

"Okay bud, give me a minute," I whisper to keep from waking Kait. As I roll out of bed, Duke gets excited, dancing around the room wagging his tail. With a grumble of annoyance, Leo rolls partially under the bed because he, like Kait, loves sleeping in.

Grabbing my robe from the dresser, I head down the hall with Duke following me into the living room and over to the sliding glass door. As soon as the door is open wide enough, he bolts out into the yard, diving into the grass. He loves sliding along the grass and this morning is no different. While he's out there doing his business, I take care of mine and then head back to the kitchen to start some coffee. Besides waking up next to Kait, it's the thing I look forward to the most every morning.

Our house is in the suburbs of Los Angeles, a densely populated bedroom community. Built in 1953 for the returning service men that were moving into the San Fernando Valley of Los Angeles. The house is sturdy and typical of the neighborhood, three small bedrooms, two baths and a decent sized backyard that Duke is currently enjoying.

My "coffee station" as Kait calls it, is in the corner of our galley kitchen. I hear the water in the kettle coming close to a boil and start grinding beans in my Breville burr grinder. Some may consider my two hundred dollar coffee grinder overkill, but not me. That's how serious I am about my coffee. With the luxury of time on weekends, I make a French press rather than brewing a pot in the coffee maker.

Back in the living room with my carafe of coffee, Duke comes darting back into the house to see what I am up to. Satisfied that I don't have any food, he plops down on the floor next to me. I enjoy these mornings because I can enjoy my coffee in peace while I watch one of the ridiculous reality shows they have about Alaska. This morning, one of my favorite gold mining shows, *Gold Rush*, is on the docket and

Duke is passed out before I fast forward through the first commercial break.

By the time Kait wakes up and heads into the living room, I've watched a couple of my shows and finished the entire French press of coffee. Leo is a few steps behind her, looking irritated that someone woke him up before noon. He slowly makes his way to the backyard giving me a dirty look before he steps through the door.

"Hey honey, have you been up long?"

"A couple hours," I say. "Do you want me to make you some coffee?"

"Oh, I would love some. Have you been watching your gold shows?"

I smile and walk back into the kitchen yelling, "Of course."

When I first met Kait I was struck by how beautiful she is. Long black hair, big eyes, athletic build and at 5'8", she's just my type. When we first started talking she told me she was looking for a guy who was at least 6'1" so I did what any guy would do and lied about my height. She loves to tease me about that fact that I'm "only" 5'11" and our whole relationship is based on a lie.

Ten minutes later with another French press full of coffee, I hand Kait her cup and refill my own. "So what time are we heading over to your parents' house today?" We're going to celebrate Mother's Day a day early so I can come back and spend tomorrow with my mother. The plan is to drive separately so Kait can spend the night at her parents' house. They live about two hours away and we don't get to see much of them these days with our busy schedule.

"I was thinking we leave here around noon so we can get down there for a late lunch, early dinner. Is there anything good on the DVR we can watch while we drink our coffee?" Kait asks.

"Let me check."

I grab the remote and scroll through the list of everything we have recorded. We have movies and shows from just about every channel available and I'm in the mood for a comedy that we can zone out to before getting on the road.

"Hey babe, what about *We're the Millers*?"

"Sounds good to me."

The movie is about a small time drug dealer, played by Jason Sudeikis, who accepts an offer to pick up drugs from Mexico and run them back across the border. He figures the best way to do this is to hire a few people to play his nerdy "family" on an RV vacation. There's no way they would stop them at the border if he was traveling in a giant motorhome with his perfect family of four. He manages to talk Jennifer Aniston's character into being his "wife," a homeless girl to be his "daughter" and a nerdy kid in the neighborhood to play his "son." The rag tag group pick up a motorhome and drive down to Mexico where antics ensue all the way back.

After the movie, we take the dogs out for a long walk. They are wiped out by the time we get home. Walking into the house, the dogs run for their water bowls. We each pull out our phones to check work email. We're expected to be on call seven days a week and need to make sure there aren't any fires to put out before we get on the road. Luckily, there's nothing urgent to deal with, so we pack up the boys' things, drop them off at my mother's house and then head out on the road for the two-hour drive.

Traffic is thin and we arrive at 1:30 p.m. When Kait's parents open the door, they're overjoyed to see us.

After our hellos, James exclaims "Let's go eat, I'm hungry!"

"Wait dad, we don't even know where we're going yet."

Kait looks at her mother and they exchange a few words in Mandarin. James and I are both "gweilo," white guys, who have no idea what the ladies are talking about.

"So Joe, how are things going at work?" James asks.

"Eh, they're good but I need to find something else. I was in New York on business last week and had an interview for a position that would be up in Northern California. They seemed to like me. I should hear back in a couple weeks about setting up a more formal interview at their offices. Might be a great opportunity. You and Lee both look great since your retirement. I'm jealous of how stress free the two of you look."

"Yeah, corporations these days try to squeeze everything out of you. You and Kait seem like you're always traveling and working too much, you need to take a break."

"I know. Speaking of which, Kait is headed to New York next week for another work conference."

"We know where we're going," Kait says as she walks over. "There's a new Thai restaurant mom wants to check out."

We all hop in James' SUV and head out for the restaurant, which is about a 30-minute drive to Temecula. James gets onto Interstate 15 and a few minutes later we pass a big

RV dealership. "Honey, look at all the RVs," Kait says. "That one looks like the motorhome they had in the movie."

James glances over as he's driving and says, "Yeah, there are a lot of those places around here. You guys want to go check out some RVs?"

"Not today dad, but maybe next time when we come for a visit? It would be fun to see what they're like inside."

"That works for me, I'm not going anywhere."

By the time we get to the restaurant, we're starving. All Kait and I had for breakfast was coffee. The place smells amazing. When we sit down, Kait and her mother scoop up the menus. James and I have learned that when we go out, the ladies do the ordering. We hang back and eat whatever is brought to the table and today is no different. After the waiter takes our order, Kait's parents start asking about how things have been and what we've been up to.

"You know, the usual. Work, work and more work," Kait says. "I have another conference next week in New York and I'll be there for four days."

"Joe was telling me about that earlier," James says. "You're going all over the country for this new job of yours."

In the nine years I've been at my company, Kait has had seven jobs. She recently started her new job as the Director of Marketing at a company that puts on conferences. The job has been challenging and she's enjoying some aspects of it, however, her workload has increased significantly leaving her with little free time.

As soon as our food arrives, Kait's phone starts buzzing. She picks up her phone, reads the message and starts rubbing her temples.

Putting my hand on her shoulder I ask, "What's the matter, babe?"

"Ericka just emailed to tell me she's quitting on Monday. I feel like I just finished training her and now I need to find a replacement. I'll give her a call when we get back to my parents' house." Kait says as she types an email back and we start serving ourselves.

"Work is so busy I feel like I can't even spend an afternoon with my family without having to deal with something at work," Kait says, looking around the table. Luckily, the Thai food is so good that, after a few minutes, Kait seems to forget about what happened and we all enjoy a great meal together.

As we walk back into Kait's parents' house, Kait heads off into the spare bedroom to call Ericka.

"Kait must work all the time," Lee says to James and me.

Sitting down on the couch, I respond, "She does. Kait gets emails at all hours of the day and is expected to respond right away. Some nights, she's working until we go to bed and back at it the minute she wakes up. It's starting to bother me, but I'm hoping things will get better for her."

A few minutes later Kait comes back into the living room and stands in front of the three of us. "I'm tired of this! Ericka is quitting without giving notice, which means she's not going to make it to the conference next week. We're already short staffed so this means I'm going to have to handle her job as well as mine. Ugh!"

I've been having a rough time at work myself, but nothing compared to what Kait has been going through. There are only nine people at the company, eight now, so it runs pretty lean. She's trying to hire people but will have to train them and simply doesn't have the time. At home, she's either on her computer or phone trying to put out fires in the office. She's working non-stop and it has been affecting our relationship.

"I think we all need a drink," I tell Kait.

"That's a great idea, Joe," James replies. "Let's open a bottle of wine."

Kait's mother doesn't drink normally, but she takes a glass that James has poured for her to join us in a toast for Mother's Day. James and I settle back onto the couch after the toast. He shares my love for these crazy Alaska shows and tunes to a new one he's found. We both laugh and make comments about the family they are portraying on the show. I don't know where they find these people but it makes for good entertainment.

Kait seems to be lost in another world with her laptop open and I can only assume that she's working. On the small table next to her I notice that her wine glass is empty so I grab the bottle and pour her a refill. She gives me a quick glance to say "thank you," grabs the glass and goes back to work.

Halfway through the Alaska show, it looks like one of the cast has somehow injured themselves by doing something stupid when Kait yells, "I can't do this anymore!"

"What now?" I ask, turning towards her.

"We should just quit our jobs, sell the house and buy an RV. We can travel around the country with Duke and Leo and enjoy life now!"

We're all stunned. I can see a mix of rage and excitement on Kait's face and I know she's not joking. "What gave you that idea?" I ask.

"I was writing an email and started thinking about the movie we watched this morning."

"You want to run drugs in a motorhome?" I ask jokingly.

"No! I was thinking about how they were traveling around in the motorhome and thought, 'Why can't we do that'? I mean, why not, right?"

"Are you serious?"

"I am serious. The more I think about it the more I like the idea. What do you think?"

"What do I think? Hmm, quit our jobs; sell the house so we can travel around in an RV without an income. I think you're crazy."

Kait's mother echoes my concern about the lack of income. Before retiring, she was a CPA and is proud that Kait and I have been working hard to develop our careers and build our retirement. I'm only 34 and as much as I would like to shuck off my responsibilities and travel, I don't want to derail all that I've worked for.

"Will you at least think about my idea?" Kait asks. She's pouring on the charm, no doubt honed over the years of being an only child. She can be convincing, and I promise her I will think about it. Remembering that I have to drive back home, I pour my glass of wine into Kait's, which is empty again, and say my goodbyes to everyone.

"Love you babe," I say as I head out to the car.

"Love you too. Are you really going to think about my idea?"

"Of course. I have a two hour drive ahead of me so there's plenty of time to think about it."

Her face lights up and she gives me a kiss.

It's dusk as I turn onto Interstate 15 and start the one hundred mile drive home. Normally on a drive like this, I would put on one of my Pandora stations and zone out, but I can't stop thinking about what Kait said. Maybe it's the romantic idea of seeing the world or maybe I am so desperate to leave my company that I can't steer myself away from this idea. It's an idea that could change our lives forever.

Neither of us has been very happy over the last few years with our work or our lives. The more we work, the more we've realized that our time is no longer our own. We've become slaves to the system. We're told what time to be at work each day, when we can leave and that we have to be available when we're not in the office. Each of us spends about three hours a day in the car driving to and from the office. The little time we do have together at night is spent decompressing in front of the TV. Then we head to bed to do it all over again. Weekends are never long enough and there's the dread of heading back to the office on Monday morning.

By most people's standards however, we're successful. We have a nice house, a couple cars, motorcycles and money in the bank. Although we're not happy at work, we have well-paying jobs that we've turned into careers with skills that will be in demand for years. We've both worked so hard to climb the ladder, how could we give that all up? What would our friends and family think? They'd call us crazy and think we were throwing our lives away on some fantasy...and maybe they'd be right.

I have to laugh because the idea is crazy. We'd be quitting our professional lives to become nomads. I've seen shows and read articles about people who have done just that. I always figured they were independently wealthy and rather than continue to work, they uprooted their lives and turned the world into their own playground. Kait can be a bit rash at times and I doubt she's even considered everything it would take to live like this. Neither of us has ever even been in an RV, let alone camped in one. How much would we be spending every month on gas, food, campgrounds and probably a thousand other things I can't think of? What would we do about health insurance? The analytical side of my brain can't stop listing all the reasons why we shouldn't do this, but my emotional side can't stop romanticizing about how good it would feel to walk into the office and tell everyone I'm quitting to live life on the road. The only thing the two sides can agree on is that we'd be taking a huge risk.

Risk. Webster defines risk as "a situation involving exposure to danger." Kids take risks all the time. It's in their nature. Pedal full speed down that steep, rocky hill? Sure, why not! Kids don't think about what happens if they lose control half way down the hill, they just go for it. As we get older the more adverse to risk we become. Our lives become predictable and easy. It's in most people's nature to settle into the routine of doing what's safe. Kait and I have been playing it safe for a while now, following the American dream to a "T."

I think back to what my father told me a couple days before he passed. Lying there in the hospital, I asked him if he had any regrets. He told me the only thing he regretted was not taking more risks. There were things he had wanted to do but never did because he was afraid to take a risk. "Don't let that happen to you," he said. "The only piece of advice I have to give you is to take risks and have a lot of children." I laughed at the last part, but he told me how much he enjoyed watching my sister and me grow up and was sad that he wouldn't be around to meet his grandchildren.

I can't stop thinking about what he said to me. "Take risks." If ever there was a risk I was going to take, this would be it. We'd be flying in the face of all conventional thinking, giving up everything that defines us as "successful" in the pursuit of happiness. Does having a lot of money make one successful or is it rather how they live their lives? Is it worth spending most of your life working just so you, hopefully, have enough money to enjoy what years you have left in retirement? I'm in my mid-thirties with a bad back and multiple reconstructive surgeries. Who knows what condition I'll be in once I reach my sixties, and it may not matter how much money we have if I'm not in shape to enjoy it.

For the first time in a long time I feel a deep sense of excitement and fear. This could all go south for us. On the other hand, we may look back and wonder why we didn't do it sooner.

I pick up the phone and call Kait.

"Let's do it!"

"Are you serious?"

"One hundred percent. I thought about how my dad told me to take risks and I think this is a risk worth taking. I don't want to look back and regret not doing this. There is a lot of planning we'll need to do before we can get on the road. I'm willing to jump off the cliff, I just would like to have a parachute in case things don't work out."

"Woo! I'm so excited and can't wait to start planning this with you. I love you so much, you don't even know!"

"You've been looking at RVs haven't you?"

"Maybe. I didn't realize they are so expensive."

"Let's not get ahead of ourselves. We have a lot to figure out before we run out and buy an RV."

"I know, I know. I'm just so excited!"

Most crazy ideas fizzle out after the excitement wears off and reality slaps you in the face, but I think this is actually going to work. I wonder how expensive an RV is?

2. FIRST RV SHOPPING TRIP

Friday, May 23rd, 2014

"Let's quit our jobs, sell the house and travel the country in an RV."

I wish it were that easy.

Kait and I just got home from work. It's been two weeks since Kait shocked me with that statement and I had no idea the amount of planning we had ahead of us when I told her I would do it. To tackle such a monumental task and keep our sanity, we broke up her statement to identify the challenges we have to overcome before we can make it a reality. The first part of that statement, "quit our jobs" is going to be one of the last things we tackle, and the most difficult. The act of walking into the office with a resignation letter is easy. Being prepared to live without income will be the challenge. Before we jump off the cliff, we need to make sure we have enough savings to get us through. How much savings is enough? That's another question we have to answer.

"So, how long do we want to travel as a homeless couple around this country?" I ask Kait.

Laughing, Kait exclaims, "We're not going to be homeless!"

"Haven't you seen all the homeless people living out of RVs down by the beach? We're going to be homeless," I respond.

"Fine. If you want to call us homeless, go ahead. Now, let's get back on track." We have a good laugh, but Kait is all business now. "We need to put together a budget so we know how much to save before we can make this a reality. I have no idea how much the RV will cost, but we can estimate most of our expenses."

"Good idea. By the way, I started doing some research and you won't believe how many people our age live in an RV and travel around the country. I found some blogs and forums of people who live this life and post their budgets. They call it 'full-time RVing.' The more I read about their adventures, the more excited I am to do this. I've been taking notes on the different RVs they travel in and am looking forward to meeting your parents to go RV shopping tomorrow."

When Kait told her parents that I had okay'd the plan, her father was beyond excited to go RV shopping with us. During my free time in the last two weeks, I have been soaking up all the information I can find on RVs. It's overwhelming how many types, models and floor plans there are to choose from. We've decided to focus on a motorhome instead of a tow behind trailer. Although there are different classes of motorhomes based on size and features, they all fall into two camps - gas or diesel. Based on my research, I convinced myself that we needed a Class A diesel pusher. These are the larger bus style motorhomes. The diesels get better mileage, ride smoother, last longer and tend to be bigger than their gas counterparts. Size is important because I think we'll need something about 38 feet or longer to live in comfortably.

I also read up on travel trailers and fifth wheels and it seems like there is more involved when it comes time to set up camp. Kait and I want to see as much of the U.S. as possible which means going to a lot of places and moving often.

With a Class A motorhome, we can access the kitchen and bathroom while we're driving. That could come in handy. Considering we haven't even seen any RVs in person, we want to focus on motorhomes first. Trailers of any sort aren't off the list; they're just at the bottom.

I'm excited to go RV shopping because we've never even been inside a motorhome. Sure, we've looked at photos and watched a few videos online, however I know that is no substitute for seeing the real thing. There are a lot of people out there living full time in their RVs, but is it for us? That thought scares me a bit. I've been fantasizing about this adventure and if it all comes tumbling down because we hate RVs, then it's going to be tough going back into the office Monday morning with our plans of living this new life down the tube.

At 6:30 a.m. Saturday morning I'm up and feel like a kid on Christmas. With coffee in hand I'd normally settle into the couch, put a gold mining show on and turn my brain off. Instead, I have my laptop open and am looking through the inventory of a few RV dealers around where Kait's parents live. We haven't figured out our budget but, brand new, the large Class A diesel pushers are a quarter million dollars and up. We don't need a budget to figure out that's well beyond our means so we'll be focused on looking for a good used motorhome and maybe pop into new units for comparison.

Manufacturers designate motorhomes by classes. Class A motorhomes can range from about 26 to 45 feet long. Class Bs are better known as camper vans. These are typically converted cargo vans for short weekend adventures. It's a class of RV we're not even considering, no way we could live in one of those. Class C motorhomes are built on a cut away truck chassis, typically Ford, and have the big box on the back with a bed in the cab over area. We haven't ruled out Class Cs, but I don't think those would work for us either.

"How long have you been up?" Kait asks as she walks into the living room rubbing her eyes looking like a sleepy panda. Duke comes running to her, tail wagging, to say good morning and to get his scratches behind those giant ears. "I've been up since 6:30 I wanted to do some more research before we head out today. I was so excited, I couldn't stay in bed."

"I know how you feel, I had trouble falling asleep last night. I was on RV Trader looking at different types of RVs. Do you think we need a big diesel motorhome? The gas motorhomes are a lot less expensive." Kait is very economical. She always says it's in her Chinese blood. Right now, I can sense her reservations about diesel pushers and I need to proceed with caution.

"Well, the gas motorhomes don't have air suspension, which means a rougher ride. The engine is upfront and I've been reading that it's loud when you are driving. Let's keep an open mind and take a look at the different RVs and see what we like, then we can worry about price."

"That sounds fair. Let me make us some breakfast then we can get going." Kait is a wonderful cook and spoils me with her creations. She doesn't cook as much lately with the demand of the new job. I'm hoping she'll get back into it more when we're traveling around the country. I guess we should add "functional kitchen" to the list of things we're looking for.

After breakfast, Kait and I drop Duke and Leo off at my mom's house again. Lucky for us she lives about 15 minutes away and is always happy to watch the dogs. Her yard is about a quarter acre and the dogs love to run around chasing squirrels. Since we don't have children, my mother considers them her four legged grandkids and like any good grandparent, she spoils them rotten. She has, however, made me promise that if we have kids, she gets to watch them as much as she watches the dogs.

When we arrive at Kait's parents' house, Lee is working on lunch. As much as I want to go straight to the dealership, Lee is making a Chinese eggplant dish that you would never find on any menu. The incredible smell has my stomach grumbling and I'm not leaving until I've had a bowl or two.

"Hey Joe!" James says extending his hand. "I've been looking at these motorhomes and they're something else. They have everything you would need to live in them." He turns toward the kitchen and says, "Honey, maybe we should get a motorhome and then we could follow Joe and Kait around the country." Lee rolls her eyes and goes back to making lunch with Kait by her side.

Two hours later we're on the road to the first RV dealership which only sells used RVs. I've learned from experience vehicle shopping with Kait, it's better for her to look at the used inventory first. If I start her off in a top of the line new motorhome, she'll be disappointed with any of the used motorhomes she sees.

"Doesn't look like anyone is here," I say as we walk out of the sales office on the RV lot. "No one's inside and I don't see anyone on the lot, but the gate is open. Let's walk around and if anyone is here they'll find us. Might be nice not to be bothered by a salesperson anyway."

"Do you think that's okay?" Kait asks.

"I don't see why not," I say over my shoulder as I head to the first motorhome I see. I can tell it's a rear diesel by the grill and radiator in the back of the motorhome. It has a silver paint job with large black swooshes and swirls on the side of it. I have no idea why companies paint their motorhomes like this. As I get closer I can see a small badge by the side door that has "38N" on it with "Fleetwood" above the door. I assume this means it's a 38-foot motorhome by Fleetwood.

Kait catches up as I am examining the exterior of the Fleetwood and asks, "What kind of motorhome is this?"

"It looks like a 38-foot diesel Fleetwood Expedition, let's see if we can go inside and take a look." I try the door and to my surprise, it's unlocked. As soon as the door starts to open, a set of stairs slides out to greet us.

"Wow!" We both exclaim at the same time. I shut the door and the stairs retract. I open and close the door a few times watching the stairs do their thing. For some strange reason, I'm in awe of the automatic steps.

"Stop playing around! Let's go inside and take a look," Kait says as she slips past me.

I follow Kait up the stairs and am surprised at the well-appointed contents of the motorhome. There is a large couch, dinette, tile floors, wood cabinets, kitchen area with a microwave, a three-burner stove and an oven. The living room feels large with the opposing slide outs. "Honey, check out the bathroom," Kait yells over to me.

I walk over and see Kait standing in the shower pretending to wash herself. "I'm surprised, there is a lot of room in here," she says. Opposite the shower, there's a door that I open to discover the toilet. Of course, I take a seat to make sure I fit in the small space. "There's just enough room in here and lucky me, I can use the toilet while you shower."

"Considering how long you take on the toilet, I'm the lucky one. I just hope there is a fan in there."

Looking up I reply, "There certainly is. I'll have to make sure I set it to the 'Taco Tuesday' setting."

I leave Kait to her faux shower and head into the bedroom at the rear of the motorhome. There is a king size bed with the headboard along the passenger side wall and a large closet in the back. Walking around the room, I open every cabinet and drawer to find that there is quite a bit of storage.

Back in the living room I find Kait going through the storage space in the kitchen and her parents relaxing on the large couch. I continue my way up to the driver's area and plop into the captain's chair. "Ahh, now this is what I am talking about." The leather chair is plush with good support on either side and makes me feel like I could drive all day. The dash has a truck like layout with the steering wheel almost perpendicular to the floor.

"Is it comfortable?" Kait asks as she walks over.

"Oh yeah. Sit down and see for yourself."

"Ahh," Kait says as she settles in the passenger seat with a very satisfied look on her face. "This is nice, I love the feel of the leather on this chair. I wonder what it's like to drive."

"I don't know. I'm almost afraid to try driving something this big."

"Me too, let's see what else they have on the lot." Looking over at her parents, Kait asks, "Do you guys want to walk around with us or stay here and wait?"

"We'll come with you," Lee says.

The lot is huge. We walk down each row, trying not to miss anything. "What did you think of that last motorhome?" I ask Kait.

"It looks pretty dated inside and I don't like the paint job. What did you think?"

"I agree that it's a bit dated, but I liked it. I feel like that size is good for us and wouldn't want to go any smaller."

"With the two boys, I don't think we could go any smaller," Kait responds.

"The problem is that we have no idea what we should be looking for in a motorhome. I saw a control panel and I had no clue what half of the switches were for. We need to learn a lot more about these things before we ever buy one."

"Agreed."

As we continue to walk through the lot, I see more motorhomes lined up next to each other. The first one is a Winnebago. I walk in with Kait right behind me. "What is that smell?" Kait asks as she puts her hand over her face.

"It smells like the people who owned this were heavy smokers, let's go look at the next one."

The next motorhome is in pretty bad shape. The door to the bathroom has come off the hinges. I see stains in the old carpet and the motorhome has an odd smell I can't place. We walk back out about as quickly as we did with the last one realizing that smell could be a big issue if we buy used.

"I think they put the nicer motorhomes up front. It looks like the ones back here are all in rough shape," I tell Kait as her parents walk up. "Why don't we head back to the car and drive over to that other dealership? They sell mostly new RVs, but they might also have some used motorhomes that we can look at." Everyone nods in agreement and as we're getting back into the car, I am shocked that we still haven't been approached by a salesperson.

The next RV dealership makes the last place look like an old used car lot. It's been a hot day so Kait's mother decides to stay in the car with the A/C running while we go look around.

"Welcome, how can we help you?" A friendly receptionist asks as we walk through the double doors. The building looks relatively new and has a large showroom floor, similar to those at a car dealership. The big difference here is that all of the RVs are in a paved back lot, which we can see through huge picture windows.

"My wife and I are looking for a motorhome and came by to see what you have," I respond.

"You came to the right place. I'll have one of our sales people come and take you around the lot. Would you care for a bottle of water while you're waiting?"

"Yes, I would love some water," Kait says to her. "And can we have one for my mom, she's waiting for us in the car."

She hands us four ice cold bottles of water and Kait takes one out to her mother while James and I look around at the accessories on display. Kait comes back in a few minutes later as the salesman walks up to us. "Hi, I'm Dave," he says extending his hand towards me. "How can I help you?"

"Hey Dave, I'm Joe and this is my wife Kait and her father, James. Kait and I are looking for a motorhome and wanted to see what you have."

"Great, do you know what you're looking for?"

"Well, we recently started looking and are considering diesel pushers 38 feet and longer, preferably used."

"Do you have a budget yet?"

"No, not yet, we're still working on putting one together."

"That's a good start. I don't have any used pushers on the lot right now, but we can take a look at some of the new units and maybe narrow down what you're looking for."

Dave leads us out the double doors into a lot packed with all different types of shiny new motorhomes and trailers. As we're walking, I see a row of motorhomes that make the used Fleetwood look like an old relic. "What are those?" I ask Dave as we walk past the first one.

"Oh that's the new Winnebago Grand Tour. It's their top of the line diesel pusher. We just got these on the lot."

"Do you mind if we check one out?"

"Not at all. In fact we should have the air conditioning in these running and it will be nice to get out of this heat." For some reason, we picked a very hot day to go RV shopping.

Dave opens the door to the Winnebago and Kait is the first one inside. "Wow, this is pretty amazing."

My jaw almost hits the polished tile floor when I walk in. This motorhome looks like a high-end luxury hotel room. The driver and passenger seats are turned towards the living room facing a large leather L-shaped couch. Directly across from the couch sits a leather recliner and a huge flat screen TV mounted above a faux fireplace. Dave must know what

I am thinking because he says, "That's an electric heater and puts out a good amount of heat. It's nice if you don't want to use the furnace. Check this out." Dave glides his hand along the side of the TV until I hear a metallic click and then he swings the TV aside to reveal a small bar.

"That's cool," Kait says over my shoulder as she walks past me to the kitchen.

The kitchen has a stone colored Corian counter top and what seems like endless storage. Dave pulls out an extension that adds more counter top space to the kitchen. Past the kitchen, Kait opens a door and says, "This even has a half bath." There is just enough room for a toilet and small sink. I slide past Kait and into the bedroom to find a ceiling fan above the king size bed and LED lights. I hop on the bed and am facing a large flat screen TV with a wardrobe on both sides and enough drawers around it to hold twice the number of clothes we own.

Stepping into the rear bath, my jaw drops again. There is a tiled shower on my left with a small bench that looks large enough for two, a large single sink along the rear wall and a toilet to my right. I open the cabinets next to the toilet and see something I never expected in a motorhome, a washer and dryer. "Babe, come in here and check this out."

Kait meets me in the rear bath, looking at me with those eyes that tell me she's in love. "We could absolutely live in something like this."

"We could, but I'm afraid to ask how much it is."

Back in the living room we take a seat on the couch with Dave and James. "So what do you guys think?" It's more of a rhetorical question, but Dave asks anyway.

"This is pretty amazing. How big is it?" I ask.

"The Grand Tour is 42 feet long and has a tag axle on the back, that's standard on anything this size."

"What's a tag axle?" Kait asks.

"A tag axle is a non-driven axle with two wheels mounted behind the drive axle, to increase handling stability."

"And how much is it?"

Dave grabs a sheet from the counter and looks at it for a second. "MSRP with all of the options, it's right around $420,000..."

In my state of shock, I miss the rest of what Dave says, but I pick up enough to hear "...of course, we can sit down and work out a price if you want to take this home today."

With a straight face, I look at Dave and say, "That's not too bad for what you get. This is our first day RV shopping so we're not ready to buy yet. We'd like to look at some of the models you were going to show us before we got sidetracked."

"I completely understand, let's head over to the other side of the lot and I'll show you the units I had in mind."

We spend the next hour looking at a couple of motorhomes that are about half the price of the Winnebago. They're nice but pale in comparison to the Grand Tour.

"Thanks for your time Dave. Kait's mother is waiting for us in the car and we need to get back," I say as we finish looking through the last motorhome.

"You're very welcome. Here's my card and if you give me your email, I can let you know when we get some used units in that match what you're looking for." I pocket Dave's card and give him my email address.

Walking back to the car, I look at Kait and ask, "So what did you think?"

"The Winnebago blew my mind. We probably shouldn't have started with the nicest motorhome they have on the lot, but I could see us living in there. None of the other motorhomes even came close to it and I didn't like the layouts as much either."

"I know what you mean. I loved that L-shaped couch and the bath and a half. It would be nice to have two bathrooms. Also, the extra four feet in length over the 38 foot motorhomes makes a big difference."

We all get into the car and as James is driving us home, I pull out my phone and start looking up used Winnebago Grand Tours. "I found a couple used ones that are a year or two old with low miles. Looks like they depreciate quite a bit."

"Oh, how much are we talking?" Kait asks with a very excited look on her face.

"Well this 2012 is about half the price of the new 2015 model we looked at."

"That's still expensive, but something to consider."

I nod my head in agreement and continue looking at listings on RV Trader for the rest of the drive. It's hard to imagine going from a 1,200 square foot house to a motorhome, but that Grand Tour certainly made it feel like it would be an upgrade. I realized two things after today's shopping experience. First, we need to figure out our budget and only look at motorhomes that fall within it. We can't keep looking at half million-dollar motorhomes because nothing else is going to compare. Second, we need to learn a lot more about motorhomes. These things have so many different components, like generators, solar systems, A/C, heating systems, black and gray tanks and hydraulic leveling systems I have no idea how to use. Even the chassis is different from motorhome to motorhome. We need a budget and an education.

3. TIME FOR A BUDGET

After a long day of RV shopping, we get to my mom's house around 8 p.m. to pick up the boys. When the dogs see us, they are so excited; you'd think that we'd been gone for weeks. I'm kneeling on the ground trying to give both boys equal attention without getting knocked over as my mother walks into the living room.

"Hey! I thought I heard you two come in, how was RV shopping?"

"Well, we found the perfect motorhome. It's just way out of our budget," I tell her.

"Show her the picture you took," Kait says as Leo nudges in closer for some more attention.

"Oh yeah, here is the living room," and I hold out my phone for my mother to see.

"That's quite something. Sounds like you two had a very productive day. The boys were great, but I am wiped out so I am going to say goodnight and head up stairs for a bath before bed."

"Love you mom," I say as I give her a hug and kiss then leash up the boys to head home.

The next morning, Kait and I wake up at the same time. It's a bit late, but the dogs don't seem to mind, especially Leo. We couldn't stop looking at motorhomes when we got home last night and didn't get to sleep until after 2 a.m. We're still laying in bed as I rollover and ask, "So, what do you want to do today?"

"I was thinking we could work on our budget. I would like to figure out how much we need to save for this upcoming adventure and how much we can afford to spend on a motorhome."

"Sounds like a good plan to me, but I need some coffee first. Would you like me to make some for you?"

"I'd love it," Kait says with a big smile. Kait enjoys coffee, but she doesn't have the love affair with it that I do.

While we're sipping on the Costa Rican coffee I roasted on my gas grill, Kait and I decide a good first step would be to better understand our current financial situation. A few years ago, we started saving money so we could make some changes to our lives. We didn't know what those changes would be, but we knew we should have as much money on hand as possible for when we were ready to make them. Adding everything we have in various accounts, we're happy with the amount of money we've put aside. However, it's not nearly enough to put a dent in that shiny new Winnebago.

"Now that we know how much we have in savings, let's figure out how much we need to budget for each month," I say to Kait.

"Okay, why don't you start a list and we'll base the figures on what we're spending now. For something like the monthly payment on the motorhome, we can estimate how much that will be."

I start putting together the spreadsheet while Kait is running down a list of monthly expenses we should include. Her list includes food, cell phone, medical, entertainment, gas, insurance and veterinarian costs for the dogs. We research costs for items like RV insurance, while estimating how many miles we will drive a month to figure out how much we'll spend on gas.

"It looks like we need about $4,600 per month. This includes everything on the list along with my guesstimates on what our monthly payment and insurance on the motorhome will be," I tell Kait as I study the spreadsheet.

"We should plan to save enough money to travel for one year without income plus a few extra months to give us time to look for jobs once we're done. Do you think one year is enough time to spend with the boys traveling around the country?"

"I think one year is perfect," I respond. "Who knows, we may hate RVing after a few months and decide to do something else."

"Very true, I guess we won't know until we get on the road and experience what living in a motorhome is really like."

"Well, based on this budget, what's the max amount we'll be able to spend on a motorhome?"

"Give me a second," Kait says as she starts typing something on her keyboard. A few minutes later she looks up at me and says, "$150,000. That's the most we can afford and still stay on budget. It's the end of May now so if we cut way back on our spending, I think we'll be able to save enough to leave by the end of the year. We could afford more motorhome if we budget less for things like food and entertainment or we work a while longer."

"I don't want to work longer," I respond. "It's going to be hard to survive until fall, let alone work longer than that. I also want to be able to go out, see things and dine at some nice restaurants while we're traveling. If we spend more on the motorhome we'll have less to do those things."

"I feel the same way, plus I think that we should try to spend a lot less than $150,000. If RVing is something we end up hating, I assume we would be able to sell the motorhome, but I don't want to take a huge loss on it. I think we should try to stay under $100,000."

"There goes the Grand Tour."

"We'll find something, don't worry honey."

It feels good to finally have a budget with a clearer picture of how much we can afford. More importantly, we have an idea of when we can leave for this year long adventure.

4. A SURPRISE AT WORK

Tuesday, June 10th, 2014

Whether I'm at home or in the office, I spend every free moment I have researching motorhomes. There are hundreds of websites and forums dedicated to the RV lifestyle. I am a sponge, soaking up everything I can learn about these things.

It has been a month since our first motorhome shopping trip and we've decided the responsible thing to do is to wait until we learn more about motorhomes before we go shopping again. Like most topics, the resources I find are people's opinion of what's best with just as many people telling them they are wrong. The more I find, the more questions I have, but I am learning a lot the further I go into the rabbit hole.

It's almost the end of the workday and I'm reading through a discussion about the pros and cons of diesel motorhomes on a popular RV forum. As I finish the page, an email notification pops up and I see something about a merger. I click the notification and start reading. It's a companywide email announcing that a competitor is purchasing our company. Before it can happen, there are all sorts of regulatory hurdles the two companies have to jump through. They estimate the merger will be complete around the end of the calendar year. "Just in time for me to leave. Who knows, maybe I'll get lucky and they'll lay me off with a nice severance package," I think to myself as I shut down my computer, pack up and leave.

Walking out of the office, conversations about the merger go from a whisper to a loud roar. Many of the people on my floor are grouped around desks discussing what this might mean for the company. As much as I would love to join in on the speculation, Kait texted me earlier to let me know she has to work late and asked if I would be able to leave a bit early so the boys weren't home alone longer than they needed to be. I throw my motorcycle gear on and head to the elevators. "Things are about to get interesting around here," I think to myself. If this goes through, it will be the fourth merger I've been through in my nine years at the company.

I get dinner started once I'm home. Leo is looking at me anxiously hoping I'll either drop something or hand him a nugget. Duke on the other hand has been standing at the kitchen window that overlooks our driveway like a sentry with his chin planted on the windowsill waiting for Kait to come home. I know when Kait is coming down the cul-de-sac because Duke's tail starts whipping back and forth. He has incredible senses and probably knew the moment she walked out of the office.

"Hey boys, I'm home!" I'm included in Kait's statement when she comes through the door, gives me a kiss and pets each of the dogs. "How was your day, honey?"

"Interesting."

"Uh oh, what happened?"

"Well, I got an email today that our company is getting purchased. There's a lot that has to happen before the merger is approved, but that's all people were talking about when I left."

"What does that mean for you?"

"I have no idea. Maybe I'll get lucky and they will lay me off."

"Don't say that. You don't want to get laid off."

"Why not? I'm going to quit at the end of the year and if I get laid off, I might get a nice severance package."

"Oh, that's right, I didn't even think about that."

As interesting as my news is, we quickly forget about it over dinner and start talking about all the places we want to see. We both want to see as many of the national parks as we can and I am particularly excited about visiting different railroad museums. I've always had a thing for trains. Kait is most looking forward to all the different food around the country and makes me promise her we'll make a stop in New Orleans.

As the weeks pass at work, the rumor mill is working overtime. Each one of my coworkers has a different theory about what is going to happen when the new company takes over. Everyone seems to be on edge because, aside from a couple vague emails, there are no details nor updates to let us know how things are progressing. We've been told to remain focused and not get distracted by rumors. The only solid information we've received is that the regulatory approvals aren't scheduled for completion until February or March of next year. I have my own theories about what's going to happen, but I'll be long gone by the time any of it comes to fruition.

Although I work in the corporate office in California, my boss and most of the people I work with are in New York. I try to get to New York as often as possible and have a drink or two with the head of our department. We've known each other since I started and despite his position, he treats me like a friend and will confide in me from time to time. I figure if there is any news worth hearing, I'll probably hear it from him before anything is made public. He rarely makes it out to Los Angeles, but I got an email from him saying that he flew in yesterday and asked me to clear my calendar at 4 p.m. so we could talk. I'm anxious because I don't know if this is simply a meeting to touch base or if he has information on the merger he wants to share with me. Either way, I'm excited to miss my weekly four o'clock status meeting to catch up with him.

The day has been dragging by. At 3:55 p.m. I grab my notebook and head down to the visitor's office. Tim is on the phone, but waves me in and points to one of the chairs across from the desk. A few minutes later he's done with the call. "Hey Joe, it's been a while. How are things going?"

"Pretty good, our projects are coming along nicely. There are a lot of rumors flying around about this whole merger."

"Yeah, I figured as much. I've been meaning to address the department and give everyone an update, but there's nothing we can tell anyone yet. They've had most of the VPs and above sign nondisclosure agreements and there are all sort of rules about what we can and cannot talk about."

"I understand. It might help to let the group know that. If nothing else, it will at least let everyone know that you're not intentionally keeping them in the dark."

"That's a good idea, I'll try to set something up via video conference once I'm back in New York. I don't have much time while I'm here and I have to leave in about 15 minutes for a dinner so let's get down to why I set up this meeting.

As you may have heard, some of the higher ups have been offered retention bonuses, myself included."

"I had heard some rumors, but nothing beyond that," I respond.

"Well, the merger committee has decided that we should extend the bonuses to essential personnel in our departments. I don't have too many of these to give out and you're one of the people I would like to offer the bonus to. In order to get the bonus, you need to stick around through the end of the merger, which from what I've been hearing, has been pushed back again."

Tim has just handed me a sheet that reiterates what he said and shows me the sizable bonus I'd receive at the end of the merger. I feel like I've been punched in the gut. I would normally be jumping up and down at the news, but if I accept, that means I'll be here for at least six months past when Kait and I plan to leave. Six months feels like an eternity to push the trip back because the only thing motivating me each morning to get up and go to work has been the promise of leaving on our adventure at the end of the year.

"Uh, thank you," is all I can muster for a response to Tim's offer.

"Is everything okay, Joe?"

"Yeah fine. Just a bit of a shock, I wasn't expecting that."

The look of concern on Tim's face has vanished with a smile and I look down at the sheet again.

"We've already lost some good people who think we're going to lay everyone off once the merger goes through. I assume you've been looking at jumping to other companies since you got that first email."

"I've talked to a few companies in the last month but nothing serious yet." A lie, but I figure this is a good cover for my initial reaction.

"If you accept, I would like to have you be part of the transition teams we're putting in place to work with the new company. This would mean signing NDAs and sticking around until the merger is completed. You won't be under contract, but you'll forfeit the bonus if you leave prior to the payout of your bonus which should come about a month after the merger."

"I understand. It seems pretty straightforward. So what do you need from me?"

"All I need is for you to tell me you will accept the offer and I'll shoot HR and your supervisor a notice that you've agreed to stay on. Once the NDAs are signed, we'll get you into the transition meetings."

"Yes, I accept and thank you so much for this, I really appreciate it." I'm not lying this time. In the brief moment I had to contemplate his offer, I realized that Tim has given Kait and me an opportunity to make our lives on the road a lot easier. Not only will we have the bonus, but we'll have at least another six months of savings to add to our account, which will give us a good security blanket.

That evening, I'm home before Kait and when she walks in door I have a bottle of our favorite red open. "I have some great news," I tell her.

"Oh? Did you get laid off today?" She asks with a huge smile.

I laugh and pour her a glass. "Not quite, remember the meeting I had with Tim today?"

"Yes."

"Well, he offered me a retention bonus that will get paid out when this merger goes through."

"That's great! Congratulations honey. When is the merger expected to go through?"

"It doesn't seem like it will go through until February or March which means I probably won't get paid out until April or even later. That means we have to stick around for at least another six months."

"How do you feel about that?" Kait asks.

"I felt sick to my stomach when Tim told me. I've been so ready to get out of here and I could see the light at the end of the tunnel. His offer pushed that timeline back quite a ways. He needed an answer right away so I told him I would agree to stay through the merger."

"What happens if you leave before the merger goes through?"

"I forfeit my bonus. In order to get the bonus, I have to stay through the merger and payout of the bonus. If I leave a day early, I don't get anything."

"You know I am okay with it either way," Kait tells me. "I know you have been dying to leave and now you're going to have to stay longer. I don't want you to do this just for the money."

"I think it might be a cool experience to be a part of the merger. Plus, with the bonus and an extra six months of savings, we will have a nice pad in case we want to travel longer or do something else after we finish RVing."

The more Kait and I talk about it, the more we both see this as a very good thing. We felt like we were rushing to do things and with our original departure date only a few months away, the decision to keep working took a huge weight off our shoulders. We still have a lot of planning to do along with buying the motorhome and selling the house.

Towards the end of the bottle, we decide to use some of the extra money to take a trip to Paris. Kait has never been and I've promised for years that I would take her.

Now we have to work on finding that one perfect mo-torhome.

5. OUR FIRST RV SHOW

Kait and I haven't been doing any motorhome shopping lately. Most of our energy has been focused on research and figuring out what kind of motorhome we want. It was fun to look at half million-dollar motorhomes, but we need to get serious and look at what we can actually afford. With all of our research, we now have a better idea of what questions to ask when we're shopping. How much horsepower and torque does the engine have? What is the towing capacity? Does it have solar and a large battery bank? Is the inverter modified or pure sine? How big are the tanks? How big are the bays? Do any of the bays have pass through storage? Is the inside living area functional when the slides are in? Are there enough outlets? With a laundry list of things to look for, it's time to get back out there and see more.

"There is an RV show in Pomona next weekend," I tell Kait as she walks into the living room. "I think we should go."

"What is an RV show like?"

"I would assume it's a lot like an auto show. The different companies will be there with their new RVs on display. I think it would be good to see what's coming out, then find local dealerships where we can go see the ones we like."

"Let's do it. After all this research, I am ready to look at motorhomes again," Kait says.

Saturday, October 11th, 2014

We get up early and make the long drive out to Pomona. October is one of the hottest months of the year in Southern California and this weekend it's in the low hundreds. I don't know why we always pick the hottest days to go motorhome shopping. When we walk through the front gate of the show, I realize my assumptions were all wrong about what goes on at an RV show. We are not prepared for what lies before us. There are endless rows of RVs from all manner of dealers. It looks like every dealer in the area has brought most of their units out to sell.

"Where do we even begin?" Kait asks.

"Let's start on the left side of the show and make our way through the dealers' displays. We should try and find some of the models we've been looking at online."

The first dealership we see is the same one we went to with Kait's parents. We spot Dave, the salesman that helped us and start heading his way.

"Let's go say hi to Dave," I tell Kait.

"Hey Joe!" Dave says as he sees me walking over.

"Dave, good to see you again," I say surprised that he remembered who I am.

"So what are you looking for today?"

"We wanted to take a look at the Grand Tour again and see if you have any other diesel pushers at the show we could take a look at."

"Great, follow me. We have a few Grand Tour layouts at the show and we'll start with the one you saw at our lot."

We follow Dave over to the Grand Tour and when we walk in, it's as nice as we remember. Although this Winnebago is way out of our price range, we're using it to make note

of the features we like so we can look for those in other motorhomes. I like the L-shaped couch. It gives the front of the
motorhome a real living room feel. Kait likes the rear bath
and we both love the king size bed. When we're done going
through the Grand Tour, we give Dave a run down of what
we like and don't like about it.

"Based on your feedback, I think I have a Thor and Fleetwood you'll like. Let's go take a look at the Thor first."

The first thing we noticed after going through the Thor
and Fleetwood motorhomes is the fit and finish isn't as good
compared to the Grand Tour. They are nice, but not on
the same level in terms of amenities. Going through motorhomes by various manufacturers back to back, we are
noticing little differences that we wouldn't have noticed if we
focused on one model, or brand, at a time. Although these
motorhomes are beyond our budget, we learn a valuable les-
son. Look at as many brands, types, sizes, and layouts as possible for comparison.

After spending time with Dave, we decide to take a break
and walk around the show to get a better idea of the inventory. Not too far from the where we came in is a huge area
of Class B camper vans. "I want to go check out a couple of
those," I tell Kait pointing at the vans.

"I didn't know Airstream made Class B vans," she says, as
we get closer to the first van I see.

"Neither did I and it looks pretty cool."

Walking around to the passenger side of the van, there is
a large awning extended to shade the outdoor furniture they
have set up. I open the large sliding door revealing the inside.
This is a Mercedes Sprinter cargo van that Airstream has con-

verted to a camper with many of the amenities of the larger motorhomes.

"Wow, I did not expect that," I say.

The front seats are turned around with a small table between the two chairs. The interior has a definite European feel to it. It's simple yet elegant. To my left is a full galley kitchen. It's small, but seems functional with plenty of space to make a meal for two. In the back, there is a couch, small TV and a few small overhead cabinets for storage. From what I can tell, it looks like the rear couch folds down to form a decent sized bed.

"There's a full bathroom in here," Kait says opening a door on the driver's side.

Poking my head in, I say, "How does that work? There's a toilet in the shower?"

"Yeah, it's a wet bath. You have to either straddle or sit down on the toilet to take a shower. Look, they even have a cover for the toilet paper so it doesn't get wet."

"There's no way I could do that," I say shaking my head. "This would be great for a long weekend or going to the motorcycle track, but we could never live in here with the boys. Where would we put all of our stuff?"

"I know you can't do it," Kait responds, "but I think I would be okay in something this small. Imagine where we could go in this. I'm sure there are places we're not going to fit in the 38-foot motorhomes we're looking at."

Sitting down in the driver's seat, I say, "You know, you make a good point. I think something like this is way too small for us, but maybe we should look at some smaller motorhomes?"

"I'd love to, but let's go find a snack first."

After our snack break, we are back on the hunt. It's starting to feel like the more motorhomes we see the more they all look alike. A giant brick with swirly lines painted on the side. As we head down another row, Kait points ahead and asks, "Which motorhome is that?"

Following her gaze, I see a yellow and white motorhome that looks like something out of the 70's. I don't see any swirls on the side. Maybe they brought out some restored motorhomes to show off? Walking closer I see a sign for the "All New Winnebago Brave."

"That looks cool," I respond to Kait. "Let go take a look inside."

We walk over to the Brave and I see that it's a gas motorhome built on the Ford chassis. Although it has a retro look, I can tell that it's just as modern as everything else we've seen. I use the term "modern" loosely because with some companies, it's hard to distinguish whether the motorhome is new or 10 years old because their designs haven't changed.

"Looks like they decided to continue the yellow and white theme on the inside as well, I kind of like it," I say to Kait as I walk up the stairs. The interior has a similar retro look that reminds me of the old movies and pictures I saw as a kid. The Brave is only 31 feet, however the opposing slide-outs make the space feel very open.

"How much is this?" Kait asks. She's standing in the center of the motorhome looking around, but seems to be keeping her distance. I can tell she's not very impressed.

"Looks like MSRP is about $120,000," I respond.

"That's a lot less than the other motorhomes we've been looking at."

"This is on the Ford gas chassis and those tend to be a lot less expensive than the diesel pushers."

"I'm not feeling it," Kait says as she sits down on the couch. "I could do this for a weekend, but I would not want to live in here. You can see the difference between this and the diesel pushers."

"Maybe we should forget about the smaller gas motorhomes because from what I've read, most of them aren't going to be as nice as the diesel pushers," I tell Kait.

"I'm good with that, let's go see what else we can find."

Not too far from the Brave is a dealer with quite a few diesels lined up. "I've read about these," I say to Kait as we walk up to one of the larger models they have. "Tiffin's are supposed to be very well made and have a great reputation for customer service."

Kait goes inside while I read the placard to try and figure out what we are looking at. "Hi, I'm Jack, can I help you?"

Turning around, I see the classic used car salesman looking back at me with a huge smile. Apparently, Jack's smile is a combination of the fact that we've stumbled upon the most expensive model they have, and the look he saw on Kait's face when she walked in the motorhome.

"Hey Jack, I'm Joe. We're just looking right now," I say trying to temper Jack's mood.

"Well I'll be around if you need anything."

"Thank you," I say and then head into the Tiffin.

"Honey, I really like this," Kait says as I walk in and see her sitting on the couch. "It's so nice."

Kait is beaming and I'm worried that Jack's instincts are right on in regards to Kait.

"Yeah, this is nice, but it's also out of our budget. I think it's more than the Grand Tour." I look around the motorhome and it seems even more polished than the luxury Winnebago we saw. For some reason, we can't seem to stay away from these luxury motorhomes.

"Do either of you know about Tiffin motorhomes?" Jack asks as he appears at the top of the steps.

"Not really," Kait says.

Jack and Kait continue talking as I make my way to the back of the motorhome. Before Jack interrupted my study of the different features, I did see that it is a 45-footer and at this length, it looks like a small house. The Grand Tour we looked at is 42-feet and the extra three feet makes an impression. This beast has tons of room.

"I would like to see a couple of your other models," I overhear Kait saying to Jack. "Great," I say sarcastically under my breath, "at least we'll get a tour." I normally don't mind sales people, however Jack strikes me as one of those salesmen who will try and pressure you into a decision by saying almost anything to make the sale. The motorhomes we are looking at probably cost about twice what our house did and it took us six months to find that. We're willing to take as much time as we need to find the right motorhome.

Kait seems pretty taken with Jack so I just follow along and stay in the background. We look at a few different models and I'm impressed with what I see. They have some interesting features, like the way the air conditioning circulates air from top to bottom to help cool or heat it faster and more efficiently.

As we walk out of the last model Jack asks, "Would you like to take one for a drive?"

"I'm kind of afraid to drive one of these, babe why don't you drive it?" Kait asks.

"Sure, I'd love to drive one."

"Great, we have a 42-foot Allegro Bus that I want to show you, but we'll have to take a golf cart over to the back lot."

We get into the cart and drive through the show towards a parking area in the back. It looks like that's where the dealers park all the overstock motorhomes. Jack drives us up to the Allegro and notices that another motorhome is blocking it in. "Let me go find the keys for this motorhome so I can move it out of the way. I'll unlock the one we're going to drive and you can take a look through it while I move this one."

"Before you go, can you turn the A/C on?" Kait asks.

"No problem," Jack responds. "Would either of you like some water?"

We both tell Jack we'd love some water and once he has the motorhome started and A/C running, we go inside while Jack disappears to find the keys.

"So what do you think?" Kait asks.

"Of the motorhome or Jack?"

"The motorhome, but do you not like Jack?"

"He's all right. I just get that pushy salesman vibe from him. It's nice that he's taking us out for a drive though. This Allegro isn't what I expected. It looks completely different with the slides in. If we find something we're serious about, we should make sure we see it with the slides in."

"Does it matter what it's like with the slides in?"

"I think it will for us. Say we're pulled over someplace and want to use the bathroom or make a sandwich. I don't want to have to put a slide out just to access the bathroom or refrigerator. We may also decide to spend a night at a Walmart and we'll want to be able to sleep with the slides in so we don't block other people or look like we've set up for a long stay."

The Allegro is cooling down quickly despite the heat and Jack is back with the keys. He moves the motorhome that is blocking our way and joins us in the Allegro. "So what do you guys think?" Jack asks.

"It's nice. Looks completely different with the slides in," Kait says.

"Well let's get out of this spot and then you can take it for a drive, Joe."

"I'm ready."

The Allegro is parked between two other motorhomes and there is very little room to maneuver a car, let alone a 42-foot motorhome. Jack jumps in the driver's seat and slaps a button on the dash. I hear the air brakes release and remember that air brakes are another benefit of diesel motorhomes over their gas counter parts. Jack slowly inches the motorhome forward and looks over at me in the passenger seat, "Check out this little trick," he says with a smile as he flicks a switch on the dashboard. "I'm raising the tag axle which will allow me to make a much tighter turn. I call it the pirouette maneuver." Once the second set of rear wheels are off the ground, he starts turning. It looks like there is no way he'll make it out of this tight spot. I'm convinced this will be the shortest test-drive in history, but he maneuvers the motorhome out on the first try and pulls it into the open to let me take over.

"Have you ever driven one of these before?" Jack asks as I slide into the driver's seat.

"I've only driven those large box trucks, never something like this."

"It's basically the same thing but longer. The main thing to watch out for is the overhang on the back of the motorhome. That tail end swings out pretty far so you'll need to give yourself some more room going around corners."

I'm a bit nervous because I'm driving about half a million dollars worth of motorhome and the last thing we need is for me to tear the roof off on a tree or flatten a car going around a corner. Speaking of which, I'm a bit shocked that, considering how much this thing is, Jack never asked for my driver's license. Pulling out onto the main road, the huge motorhome accelerates very smoothly and seems to have quite a bit of power. I'm surprised at how quiet the cab is with the engine in the back. As soon as I finish the turn, my nerves settle.

"This is very easy to drive, you sure you don't want to give it a try?" I ask Kait.

"No, I'm good riding back here, plus I get to see what it's like if we have passengers."

Jack directs me onto the busy 10 Freeway and I am impressed with how quickly the motorhome is able to get up to speed. The side view cameras make merging into traffic a lot easier than I thought. I'm also reminded that this is as tall and almost as long as some of the trucks around me.

"I'm amazed at how smooth the ride is," I say to Jack as we're cruising along the freeway.

"There is a lot of rattling back here," Kait says. "Is that normal?"

"You're always going to get some rattles and we can address those before you take delivery of the motorhome."

That's when Jack hits me with the question I've been dreading. "So what do you think?"

"I like it, but I'm not sure if this would be the right motorhome for us."

"Well what if I was able to offer you an amazing price on this motorhome, would you consider buying today?" Jack seems to be getting that excited look on his face again. We're almost back at the show and I can tell that a simple "no" isn't going to work for him.

"Not today. We recently started looking at motorhomes and we have a lot to see before we make a decision."

"Look, I get it," Jack responds. "But I can offer you an amazing deal on this that you're not going to find anywhere else. You're welcome to think about it, but this unit probably won't be here in a day or two."

I drive back into the auxiliary lot, park the motorhome and turn to face Jack. "I understand. We're just not ready to buy anything, especially something as expensive as this. Give me your card and when we get closer to making a decision we'll give you a call," I say as I get out of the driver's seat.

Jack's mood has gone from happy and helpful salesman to plain angry. He pulls a card out of his pocket and mutters a goodbye as we step out of the Tiffin. He doesn't bother to follow us or offer to drive us back into the show.

"He didn't seem too happy about my response," I say to Kait as we start walking back to the main gate.

"No, he didn't and I'm not going to be pressured into buying something like that. I mean, he's acting like we're shopping for a new phone and not something that costs more than most houses. It's not like we begged him to drive the thing." Kait looks like she's stewing at this point so I decide to let her cool down.

Once we make it back into the show, Kait's calmed down and asks, "So how did you like driving it?"

"I was impressed at how easy it was to drive. All that worrying for nothing."

"I was surprised how smooth the ride was," Kait says. "I can see us driving something like that all over the country. I know gas motorhomes are less expensive, but I feel like we would be so much more comfortable in a diesel."

"I completely agree. Is there anything else you want to see?"

"No, I'm tired and really hot. Why don't we head home, go get the boys and have a nice dinner."

"Sounds good to me."

Although it wasn't quite what we expected, the RV show went well for us. We learned a lot and have a much better understanding of the different sizes and types of motorhomes available. It helped to have so many different brands and models to walk through, but at the same time it was completely overwhelming. In the end, I think we came away with a clearer understanding of the type of motorhome and features we want.

6. THE MECCA OF RVs

Shortly after the RV Show, I kept my promise to Kait and took her to Paris for our anniversary. I spent quite a bit of time in France when I was in high school on an exchange program and I was excited to show her around the City of Love. Kait is a die-hard foodie. Instead of visiting The Louvre or Musée d'Orsay, we made reservations at some of the best restaurants in town. To say we ate our way through Paris would be an understatement. It was a fun getaway and a well needed break for both of us. Once we got home, we were ready to get back to planning our new life and walk off those extra pounds at RV dealerships.

With a diesel pusher in our sights, we've realized we can't afford a new one. Kait and I have been spending our evenings scouring the Internet for used motorhomes that we like, sitting together on the couch looking through ad after ad. The funny thing with online ads is that some do a great job showing the motorhome in detail while others only show a picture of the outside.

As we start another night of online shopping, Kait asks, "Where do you think the best place is to shop for used motorhomes?"

"Hmm, good question. My guess would be Florida. Big retirement community and I would think there are a lot of lightly used, well taken care of motorhomes down there. Let's look online and see what we find."

In the last hour, not only have we found hundreds of motorhomes in Florida, but many of them are located at one particular dealership. A quick online search reveals that they claim to be the "Largest RV Dealership in the World."

"Check this place out, they have almost everything," I say turning my screen towards Kait. "It's not too far from Suzanne and Rick's place in central Florida. Maybe we can visit with them and get a rental car to drive down to the dealership." Suzanne and Rick are my brother-in-law's parents and we enjoy their company quite a bit.

"That's a good idea, why don't you text Suzanne and ask if we can come visit? My Aunt and Uncle don't live far from there either, maybe we can visit them as well?"

"Sounds like a great plan to me."

Friday, December 19th, 2014

We just landed in Orlando, Florida and rented a car to drive to Suzanne and Rick's place outside of Ocala. The plan is to spend a few days with them then drive back to the Orlando area to spend Christmas with Kait's Aunt and Uncle.

Suzanne and Rick have a large ranch in central Florida that I have been to a few times. It's a gorgeous property with huge oak trees covered in Spanish moss. They have a long driveway up to their property and as we're making our way towards the house, Kait can't stop admiring all the fields we pass. "They have horses. Oh look, they have donkeys too!" Kait exclaims.

"Oh, wait till you see their chickens and the coop they built. It looks like a nice guest house."

"I can't wait, do you think we'll get to eat any of the fresh eggs?"

"I'd be surprised if we didn't," I respond as we pull up to the front of the house.

Suzanne and Rick greet us with glasses of wine as we walk through the front door. They both have great taste in wine and love to share. We set our luggage down in the guest room and head back to the main house after getting settled. It's about 7 p.m., Suzanne has dinner ready for us and Rick has another bottle of wine open. We spend a good portion of the evening answering questions about the one year adventure we're planning and the motorhomes we're looking at. Susanne and Rick tell us that they have also been considering a motorhome and we decide to go RV shopping together.

"What are you guys planning to do for money while you're on the road?" Rick asks.

"We've been saving so we'll have enough money to be on the road for a year. If we love it and want to keep going, we'll need to figure something out," I tell them.

"I'm so excited for you two," Suzanne says. "It's great that you are doing this now and not waiting until you're older."

After dinner, we're wiped out and make plans to head out early in the morning, stop in at a few motorhome dealerships on the way down to the "World's Largest."

The next morning, Kait and I walk over to the chicken coop to collect eggs for Suzanne so she can make her famous omelette. After breakfast and coffee, we all pile into Rick's car and make our way south. The first dealership we stop at is one that Rick recommended. When we park, I look across the lot and see a brand new 45-foot Monaco and break my own rule of staying out of motorhomes we can't afford. This thing is amazing, but before I get too attached I hear Kait yell, "Hey babe, we're here to shop, not daydream. Rick is coming over with a salesman."

The salesman's name is also Joe and he seems to be more my type, laid back and willing to listen. We tell him we're looking for used diesel pushers between 38 to 42-feet. "No problem, I have a very nice motorhome in the back lot."

We follow Joe to the back lot where he shows us a 42-foot 2007 American Coach Eagle. It's older than what we're looking for and on the high end of our budget, but we figure there's no harm in taking a look. The Eagle doesn't look its age and it's apparent that the previous owners took good care of it. "If you're looking for used units," Joe says, "you want to stay away from ones made after the 2008 crash. A lot of manufacturers were going out of business and those that survived were cutting a lot of corners. They only started getting good again in the last few years."

"I wouldn't have thought about that, but it makes a lot of sense," Rick says.

We take a look at a few other units before we thank Joe and get back in the car. We had a few other stops planned, but given the time, we decided to head straight for the "World's Largest." If this dealership is as big as they advertise, we will probably need most of the day there to look through all the motorhomes.

Getting off the highway, the dealership looks bigger than it did online. In the few minutes it takes to drive around to the main entrance, we truly get a sense of how large this dealership is. It looks like they converted an old RV park because these RVs aren't stacked on top of each other and are sitting on their own pads with grass and trees in-between. I'm not in the mood to deal with another salesperson so I tell the receptionist we'd like to look around on our own. "Sorry, but we have so many units here that you'll need someone to show you around, otherwise you won't see half this place. If you'd like, we have a cafeteria and you can grab a complimentary coffee or bottle of water while you wait."

Before the receptionist is even done speaking, I'm heading toward the cafeteria on a quest for the nectar of the gods. Although I am a connoisseur, at times like this any cup of that brown magic liquid will do. The cafeteria is huge and looks like they're set up to feed a small army. The food looks tempting but I head straight for the coffee station, fill up a cup and stuff a few bottles of water into my pockets for everyone. With my coffee in hand and my pants about to fall off from the weight of the water, I find everyone talking with the salesman. "Joe, this is Jason," Kait says.

"Hi Joe," Jason says extending his hand. "Your wife told me what you guys are looking for. Do you mind my asking what your budget is? I ask because we have motorhomes that go all the way up to a million or more and I don't want to waste your time."

Before coming out to Florida, Kait and I discussed that we would not share our budget with the salespeople. If they know our budget, they would know how much we plan to spend and could use that against us when we sit down to negotiate.

"We have a budget in mind Jason, but not something we want to share right now. I can say that million dollar rigs are well beyond our budget. We're looking for a used DP in good condition, but if you have something else you think we might like, we're open to take a look."

"I've got some older units that are in nice shape I think you'll like. Let me grab a golf cart and we can head out."

They have an armada of six-seater golf carts waiting to shuttle people around. We all get in and head to one of the lots away from the main building. It takes us a few minutes to make it to the first motorhome and on the ride over we probably saw every type of RV sold in the country. They have rows and rows of trailers, fifth wheels and all types of motorhomes.

"This is a 2004 Monaco Dynasty," Jason says as he unlocks the motorhome. "It's been well taken care of and listed at $165,000, but don't worry about that, we can always sit down and work something out on the price. I'll wait out here so you can look through the Monaco without me bothering you. If you need anything just holler."

The Monaco is nice, but it feels dated, especially with the tube TV mounted above the driver's area. Having looked at high end motorhomes at the RV Show, we are a bit spoiled. Rick and Suzanne follow us inside and I can tell Suzanne isn't too impressed. "This looks pretty beat up," she says to Rick. "If we got something like this, I would want to gut it and redo everything."

Kait looks over at me and nods her head in agreement. The size and layout are nice, but at this price we won't have any money to upgrade the interior. Jason looks up from his phone as we make our way out and asks, "So what did you think?"

"It's a bit too dated for us, do you have anything newer?"

"I do but those units are going to be much more expensive. Would you like to see those? Otherwise I could show you some gas motorhomes or something that's not quite as long?"

"Sure, let's see the smaller options," Kait says back to Jason.

On the way to the next motorhome, Rick asks Jason to show him and Suzanne one of the higher end used motorhomes. Jason nods and turns down the next aisle, pulling up next to what looks like a tour bus.

"Wow, what is that thing?" I ask.

"This is a 2005 Prevost Liberty. It just got turned in to us and is in great shape. The previous owners used to go to classic car shows and they would pull a double stacked trailer with a couple of the cars they showed."

Suzanne is nudging Rick as her face brightens and she says under her breath, "This is what we need."

Jason waits for us in the golf cart again while we all go inspect the Prevost. Suzanne and Rick know someone with a Prevost and told us the "st" is silent and it's pronounced "Prevo." The motorhome is absolutely amazing. According to Jason these retailed for close to two million new and he considers this one to be a steal at $549,000. The high price tag is because these are built on a Prevost bus chassis, and then customized by a luxury bus conversion company, in this case it was done by Liberty Coach. As nice as some of the high-end motorhomes we've seen are, they pale in comparison to the Prevost. Kait and I can't get over how nice it is. "I wonder if we could find an older one in our price range?" Kait says to me.

"I'm sure we can, but it's going to be pretty old and probably need a lot of work. I can't imagine what it costs to maintain one of these."

In the rear bedroom of the Liberty, there are mirrors everywhere and the bed has a somewhat rounded shape, but I don't see a door. Looking around, I spot a small panel next to the entrance that has two buttons labeled, "Door Open" and "Door Close." I press the close button and instantly hear a hydraulic "whoosh" as a hidden pocket door flies closed. "Wow!" Pressing the open button, I hear the same noise and the door opens. "Babe, come in here."

Kait joins me in the bedroom and I point to the button, "Push that."

"Ahhh!" Kait screams. "That scared me, I was not expecting the door to fly closed like that."

"It's like something out of *Star Wars*. And I thought the automatic steps were cool."

Back in the living room, Suzanne has found her favorite feature - a fifty-bottle wine cooler. "This is what we need when we get a motorhome," she says.

After we finish oohing and aahing over the Prevost, Jason drives us to the next motorhome. It is another Monaco, but different than anything else we've seen. Although it's used, it looks more streamlined and modern than the other used motorhomes we've seen. "Is this gas?" I ask Jason as we pull up next to it.

"No, it's a front engine diesel. This is a 2012 Monaco Vesta 35-footer. It's a few feet shorter than what you're looking for, but I think you'll like that it's more modern than that '04 we saw."

The Vesta is mid-entry so when you step in, you're in the living room rather than the driver's compartment. A bit of living area is lost due to the entry, but the layout is very nice. Jason was right; the interior is definitely more modern than some of the other used motorhomes we've looked at. With a rounded and sloped front end, the driver's compartment almost feels like I'm in a space ship. There is a step up to the driver and passenger seats with a nice commanding view of the road.

"It's smaller than what we've been looking for, but I think it could work for us," I say to Kait.

"I really like it, did Jason say how much it is?"

"No, let me go ask him," I say as I walk outside.

"Jason, how much is the Vesta?"

"Uh," Jason says looking down at an inventory sheet. "Asking is $200,000."

I go back in and tell Kait how much it is and she jokingly responds, "Should we tell him we'll give him a $100,000 cash and see what says?"

"Sure, if we had $100,000 in cash," I say smiling back at her. "Want to take it for a drive?"

"Okay, but you drive again. I'm not ready to drive one of these yet."

"I guess all those years of driving big box trucks after college is finally coming in handy," I say smiling at Kait.

We take the Vesta out and it drives more like a van than a large motorhome. It's definitely not as smooth as the Tiffin, but it still has a nice ride. I do notice that the 300 horsepower engine is more sluggish and it takes more time and effort to get up to speed on the highway. With the engine upfront, there is also more noise, but it's not annoying.

We like the Vesta, but even if we're able to negotiate a better price, it's still well above our budget. I don't know too much about Monaco as a brand, but I am concerned that this particular model was only made for two years. It could be difficult to find parts if and when we have any issues. However, I have made a mental note to look into other front engine diesels when we get home.

Jason also showed us some gas motorhomes, but we didn't see anything we liked. Worn out from the long day of shopping, we were all ready to call it a day. Suzanne and Rick recommended a steakhouse nearby and we agreed it would be nice to sit down and enjoy a meal together. Kait was the most excited. I could tell that our shopping trip was starting to take its toll on her and there's nothing like the mention of good food to perk Kait up. Plus, I could go for a huge slab of beef.

Over the course of our weeklong stay in Florida, we visited a few more RV dealerships. Most of the diesel motorhomes in our budget are about 10 years old and well worn. Since we'll be living in the motorhome full time, we are looking at them similar to a house. Imagine buying a house that came completely furnished with a used bed, couch and everything else that was 10 years old. Sure, you can swap out the mattress and other things, but it's going to cost you quite a bit. That's something that is bothering us about these older and well used motorhomes.

7. FINDING THE PERFECT TOAD

Saturday, January 3rd, 2015

Although we don't have our motorhome yet, Kait and I decided it was time to start shopping for a "toad." A toad is a car that can be towed behind the motorhome. This way, we don't have to go grocery shopping in a 42-foot motorhome. I can't imagine trying to pull into a Whole Foods parking lot with that beast, let alone finding a place to park it. The tricky thing about shopping for a toad is that there are a limited number of cars that can be towed with all four wheels on the ground. As luck would have it, neither of our cars can be flat towed and we don't want the hassle of using a trailer to tow one of the cars. Many of the American brands have flat towable vehicles, so we've decided to take a break from motorhome shopping to go toad shopping.

"Let's put together a list of things we want in a toad," I tell Kait.

"Well, we need to have enough room for the boys and it should be easy for Duke to get into since his hips are starting to bother him." I'm busy taking notes while Kait is talking, "And we should probably have room for passengers."

"I think we should have something that's four-wheel drive," I add.

"Why do we need four-wheel drive? When we shopped for the Grand Cherokee you specifically said we don't need it in a four by four."

"I'm envisioning some of the off grid places we might camp. I think it would be great to have a car we can take on the trails and use to explore the area."

"That's a good idea. Let's add four-wheel drive to the list," Kait tells me.

A couple hours later, I've narrowed down a list of vehicles we can shop for. Three of them are four-wheel drive and two are standard cars.

"Let me ask you. If we had bought the Grand Cherokee in four by four, would we be able to tow it and not have to get a new car?" Kait asks.

"Yes. But would you want to take our Cherokee on some of the trails I'm thinking of?"

"Good point," Kait responds.

Saturday, January 10th, 2015

We are up early and start at the Ford dealership. Two of the cars I found are Fords and I am curious to see what Kait thinks. "So which two cars are we looking at?" Kait asks.

"The Explorer and the Flex."

"Flex? What is that?"

"That's a Flex," I say pointing across the lot.

"What is that, a station wagon?"

"Kind of, I figured it would be great for long trips with the boys and we could fit a lot of stuff in it. The thing is huge and you can get it in all wheel drive. Let's at least go take a look."

We walk over to the Flex and I hop into the driver's seat. "This is comfortable and there is a ton of room in here."

"I'm good." Kait's standard response when she's not into something. "We don't need a car this big and it's not my style."

I expected this reaction so I walk Kait over to option number two. "The Explorer looks nice," Kait says. We spend some time checking out the different options, trim levels and price tags. "Wow, this one is over $50,000!" Kait exclaims a few cars over. These are more expensive than I expected. The Explorers on the lot with four-wheel drive are in the high 30's to low 40's. That's more than what we want to pay, especially for something we're going to tow behind a motorhome and drive off-road.

With Ford crossed off our list, we head to the Fiat and Subaru dealerships. These cars are more in line with our budget, but we can only flat tow them if they have a manual transmission. I grew up driving a stick shift, but Kait refuses to get one. Our options are starting to narrow, but I have an ace up my sleeve.

"So what cars do they have that are flat towable?" Kait asks as we pull into the Chrysler Jeep dealership.

"They have a few models, but I think based on what we're looking for, the Wrangler might be the best option."

"Don't they ride rough?"

"I don't know. The new models are supposed to be much smoother and more refined. Why don't we go check out a couple?"

"Okay, but only because I know you've wanted a Wrangler since you saw 'Jurassic Park' as a kid."

She knows me too well. The Wrangler has been my dream car for a long time and it's hard to contain my excitement. We walk up to a row of Wranglers and Kait starts studying the sticker. "I didn't know Jeeps were this expensive. This one is over $40,000!"

"That's the Rubicon model. We should look at the Sport model. Look, this one is under $30,000," I say as I point to a barebones Sport. "I kind of like this. I haven't seen roll up windows in a long time," Kait says as she opens the door to the Jeep and peers inside. "This is manual. Can we tow an automatic?"

"We sure can, you can tow any of these," I say with a sweeping motion towards all of the Wranglers.

"Can I help you two with anything?" I hear as the salesman approaches.

After we make our introductions, the salesman shows us the different trim levels they have for the Wrangler. Kait and I decide that a Sport S is the best option for us. We like the four-door model with larger tires, automatic windows, hardtop and, of course, automatic transmission.

"Why don't you take it for a drive?" The salesman says to us. When we hop in, Kait asks how the roof works. "You can remove the entire roof if you want to, or just the two panels up here in the front," he tells her.

"Can we see how they come off?" she asks.

"Of course."

The three of us have the panels off in a couple of minutes and Kait takes the Wrangler out first. I'm next up in the driver's seat. Out on the road, I find that the Wrangler's ride is a lot better than some of the older Jeeps I've been in.

Back at the dealership, Kait and I step away to talk about the Wrangler. "So what did you think?" I ask Kait.

"I like it, but I'm not ready to buy one. Do we have to buy new or can we look at some used ones?"

Although my hopes of driving home with a brand spanking new Jeep have been dashed, I'm excited because Kait likes it. "Absolutely. We don't need to buy it today."

Over the next few weeks, I scour the Internet in search of used Wranglers in good condition. It turns out to be a lot harder than I expected. Most used Wranglers have lifts, beefy steel bumpers, or various other things the owner added to them. I'd prefer to buy one that's stock, but those seem to fetch a premium.

"How's the search coming for your Jeep?" Kait asks as I'm back on my laptop ignoring whatever sitcom is currently on TV.

"I'm finding a lot of Jeeps, but the few that are still stock cost almost as much as the new ones. Wranglers have one of the highest resale values out there."

"Then why would we buy used?" Kait asks.

"I have no idea. I say we get something new, that way we don't have to worry about inheriting someone else's problems. Want to go back to that dealer tomorrow and see if we can find something?"

"Sure, let's do it!"

Kait seems genuinely excited about getting the Jeep, but she keeps referring to it as "your Jeep." I'm not going to complain. The next day we're back to the dealership and it looks like they have about half the Wranglers we saw last time. We find the same salesman we spoke to and I ask if they still have the "Tank" green Wrangler that we test-drove.

"Sorry, unfortunately we sold that one shortly after you drove it. Those Tank colored Jeeps fly out of here. The only Wranglers we have are the ones out there on the lot," the salesman says pointing to the Jeeps we just walked past. "We're expecting a shipment soon and I can call you when they arrive."

"Are any of the ones you have on the lot the four door Sport S model with automatic transmission, hardtop and tow package?"

"Yes, that blue one has those same options."

I turn towards the row of Wranglers and see the only blue Jeep sitting there. It looks exactly like the one we test-drove except for the color. "Does the color matter that much? I mean, it's a Jeep right? Maybe I'll get used to the color and grow to love it," I think to myself.

There is a completely illogical debate going on in my head driven by more than twenty years of lusting after this exact vehicle. Kait was right. When I saw "Jurassic Park" as a kid, I fell instantly in love with the Jeeps in the movie. As I grew up, I envied friends who had them and kept telling myself I would get one someday. When Kait and I bought our first car together, I thought about pushing for the Wrangler, but we wanted something more refined, so we got a Jeep Grand Cherokee complete with seat warmers. It seemed like my wish to one day have a Wrangler was long gone, until now. Standing there in front of the blue Wrangler, I realize I've lost all rational thought and I am ready to yell, "I'll take it!" when I feel a hand on my shoulder.

Kait knows me well. Very well. "Honey, look at me. You don't want a blue Wrangler. We don't have to buy anything today."

It feels like reality slapped me in the face and I come back to my senses. "You're right," I tell her. "You know me, I don't like waiting when it comes to stuff like this."

"I know." Kait turns to the salesman and asks, "When does your shipment come in?"

"Should be here in a week or two. Hard to say exactly when, but it doesn't look like we'll be getting any of the Sport S models in the Tank green color. If you want, you can special order one with all the options and colors you want, it will just take about five weeks to show up."

I'm not sure I can handle five weeks, but it's good to know we can order exactly what we want. As we're getting back into the Cherokee, Kait says, "Why don't you see if there is another dealership around here that has any Tank colored Jeeps?"

Why didn't I think of that, of course! Hope that I'll have a Tank green Jeep parked in the driveway this evening has flooded back into my mind as I look up the next closest dealership. To my amazement, they have the exact Wrangler I'm looking for. When I call the dealership, they confirm it's still there. Based on what the last salesman said about the Tank green Wranglers flying off the lots, I give myself a 50/50 chance that it's still there when we arrive. Yes, the illogical side of my brain has kicked in again.

Arriving at the second dealership, I spot the green Jeep before we're even parked. I'm in my mid-30s, but feel like a kid again. I ask Kait to see if she can wrangle, no pun intended, up a salesman while I check it out. I don't need to see it to know it's the one I want, but I see another couple walking around it. In my child like state, I am wondering if licking the Jeep would signify the same claim to ownership as it did when I was a kid on the playground.

Kait seems to reach the Wrangler before I do with a salesman in tow. "Is this the Wrangler you are looking for?" She asks. Her tone tells me that she's taking over at this point. "Yes that's the one."

She turns back towards the salesman and states, "This is the Jeep we'd like to test-drive."

This Wrangler is exactly what I am looking for, right down to the Tank green color, which is reminiscent of the original Willy's Jeeps from World War II. The symbolism isn't lost on me.

When we get back to the dealership, Kait pulls me aside. "Look, I like the Jeep, but I am not paying anything more than this," she says holding up her phone so the salesman isn't able to see. I notice a figure, which is quite a bit less than the sticker price. Full blown panic has set in. "That's too low, we'll never get the Jeep for that," I say. "I've been researching how much these sell for and that's lower than anything I've seen."

There's no emotion on Kait's face. I know she wants, more than anything, for me to get the car of my dreams, but that fact has been buried somewhere deep in her head. The "Price Terminator" standing in front of me now is unwavering. "It's this price or we walk."

While I'm normally as cool as a cucumber when it comes to these kinds of things, I am on the verge of a full-blown meltdown. My dream car has been dangled in front of me and I suddenly see it vanish from view because of the impossibly low, take it or leave it price, Kait is demanding.

"Why don't you wait in the car and let me handle this," the Price Terminator says. "I'll be back."

"Uhh, I'd probably screw things up anyway," I stammer.

As Kait heads into the dealership, I pull my iPhone out and start going back through all of my research on pricing for Wranglers. Maybe I was misremembering and Kait's price is right on. Scrolling through a few different websites I realize I am right. There's no way we're walking out of here today with the Wrangler. A strange calm has come over me from my conclusion and then the passenger door opens.

"Time to come inside honey, we're getting a Wrangler," Kait says. I can tell she's trying to suppress a smile, but it's not working.

"Are you serious?"

"Yep," she says very nonchalantly. "They had to bring the sales manager over to talk to me, but he agreed to my price." She finally allows herself to smile. "I'll tell you all about it later."

I can't explain how excited, happy, relieved and, quite honestly, shocked I am. Somehow Kait managed to pull it off. Pulling myself together, I get out of the car and hand the keys over to a waiting salesman. Kait tells me he needs to take our Grand Cherokee because they also agreed to her price for the trade-in. I'm speechless as we walk inside and sit down with the sales manager. He gives me a look that I've seen before when Kait has worn someone down. I can't help but feel a little bit sorry for the guy. I've seen Kait in action and never want to be on the other side of the negotiation table.

"Okay," the sales manager says as he slides a piece of paper across the desk. "Here is the price we agreed on plus tax, title and license and this is your balance after we deduct the value of your trade-in. Would you like to finance or pay outright?"

"We'll pay outright and do you have some type of certificate or something for the $500 discount you said you'd give me on parts and service?"

Confused, the sales manager says, "I never agreed to that."

"Huh, I thought you did," Kait says. "I thought that was part of what I was agreeing to when we spoke. I must have misunderstood you. Since it's not part of the deal, this won't work for us."

Panic. I thought this was a done deal and I turn to Kait with a "What's going on?" look, but she doesn't look away from the sales manager.

"Look, I'll take another $300 off the price if we can just shake on this deal now and call it a day," the sales manager says with the look of a broken man.

"Deal." Kait says with a huge smile. Not only have I gotten the Wrangler I wanted, but Kait got it at a price $300 less than what I already thought was impossible.

Over an hour later, we're sitting in the lounge waiting for them to finish getting our, I mean my, new Wrangler ready. Leaning closer to Kait I whisper, "I've been meaning to ask you. What was that all about when you told the sales manager that you were expecting $500 worth in parts?"

"Oh, that. In all the excitement I completely forgot to fill you in. When I was negotiating I told him that I wanted a $500 discount on any parts and service. I figured we might need some stuff for the Jeep. Since he didn't say no, I assumed he agreed to give us the credit and when he said he didn't, I was willing to walk away."

"I know and I almost soiled my pants!"

"Well it worked out and you got your Jeep. Congratulations!" Kait says with another huge smile.

8. SECOND GUESSING

Wednesday, February 18th, 2015

I am ready to start living our new life. The merger at work was supposed to be well on its way to completion, but it seems that every few weeks there is a new rumor about the merger being pushed back and that it may not even go through. Some of the rumors are simply that, but others are being validated by news stories about the two companies. The net result is that company morale is quickly going down the tubes and all of the "focus on the task at hand" speeches are doing more harm than good.

This week has been particularly bad. I've been tasked with putting together a report that the executives need for a sit down meeting with the new company. Apparently they want to see how similar our systems are and my role is to defend the what, how and why we do things a certain way. I see some of the flaws on our side and think there are some real benefits to how the other company does things. It's more about politics than anything else, and I hate politics.

Maybe it's the week I'm having, but I'm starting to get stressed about our idea to get out on the road. I want to be out of here but at the same time, doubt has crept into my head about whether this is the right idea. I'm making great money and they seem to value what I do. If I stick around I could have a great career with the new company, but is that what I want? Or am I a fool for walking out on what looks like a great thing, at least on paper? I think these questions are nagging at me because I am also starting to get stressed about the execution of our plan. I feel like we're going in circles trying to find the right motorhome. We still have to get the house ready to sell and there are about a thousand other things on my list of to-dos.

After my hour and a half drive, I'm finally home and ready to shut my brain off. I know I have other things I need to do but instead I turn on the TV. Leo jumps up on the couch with me and Duke crawls into my lap.

Whenever I am stressed, the boys seem to need more love than usual. After five minutes of petting the two of them, I feel a hundred times better. I can see the truth in all those articles that talk about how dog owners live longer.

An hour later, Duke's head erupts off my lap and he goes running to the kitchen window. I hear Kait walk through the door and she's greeted by two tails wagging out of control. "How was work, babe?" I ask.

"I don't know how much more of this I can take. Another person quit today. I don't have time to do my job AND train a new person every few weeks. This is ridiculous. I don't want to talk about work anymore. How was your day?"

"It's been a rough week, but I decided I'm not going to answer any emails tonight and just relax. I need some time to turn my brain off. I'm getting stressed about everything."

"Work or our new life?"

"Both. Work has been tough and I'm having doubts about what we're doing which is making me nervous about walking away from my career."

"That makes sense, but what's the worst that can happen? We hate it, spend all of our savings and end up living at your mom's house?" I nod my head at Kait as she continues on.

"It's not like the world is going to end. We can get other jobs, we can buy another house, but we may never have a chance to do something like this again. I don't think anyone has ever been laying on their deathbed wishing they had worked more. We're taking a huge risk and making a change in our lives. It's perfectly normal to be nervous about that. Remember that we're taking a calculated risk and not just jumping off the cliff, hoping this works. We've made a plan that includes a net for ourselves if things don't work out. But, if you realize that this is something you don't want to do, I will support you 100%."

Kait's right. I realize that I've lost sight of why I agreed to do this in the first place. To take risks and redefine what success means to me. I think back to when I told Kait I would go on this adventure with her. I realized then that the money, the house, the career isn't what makes me successful. Success for us is living a happy fulfilled life on our terms and right now that means being able to spend quality time together traveling around the country with the boys. This is an opportunity for me to take the risk of leaving it all and make a meaningful change in my life to be truly happy and successful.

I also realize that I've become too wrapped up in material things, thinking I always need more. Now I'm finding the opposite to be true. As we plan to get rid of most of our stuff and leave the rat race, I'm finally starting to feel free. Free from the things that have weighed us down and the obligations we had so we could get more. We're not there yet, but Kait has helped me to see the light at the end of the tunnel.

I had been holding back from saying anything to Kait about my doubts because I was worried she might get upset that I was thinking of calling the whole thing off. A huge weight has been lifted off my shoulders, not only to vocalize what has been causing me a number of sleepless nights, but to also have Kait tell me that she supports my decision either way. Any doubts I had about leaving our careers behind and hitting the open road have evaporated.

9. NEW FRIENDS, NEW DIRECTION

Thursday, March 5th, 2015

When we came up with the idea for our new life, we thought it would be cool to start a blog and share our experiences. It was going to be this groundbreaking idea and people would be astonished by what we were doing. That concept quickly faded as I began my research and found blog after blog of people our age doing exactly what we were looking to do. I connected with one couple's blog, Dean and Patricia, who seemed very much like us. They had quit their conventional careers and were now traveling and working on the road full time. As I was going through their blog, I saw that they were going to be in the Los Angeles area and decided to send them an email. I let them know that I am a native of Los Angeles so if they had any questions about the area to let me know.

"I just got an email from Dean and Patricia. They'll be down by your parents' next weekend and want to know if we'd like to meet them at their motorhome for the day," I tell Kait.

"I'd love to. Where are we going to meet them?"

"They are staying at a winery out there. They said it's part of Harvest Hosts."

"Is that the program you were telling me about that allows RVers to boondock at their business?"

"Yep, that's the one. I'm excited to see what their motorhome set up is like. Aside from the motorhomes we've seen for sale, we've never been in one that people are living out of full time."

Saturday, March 14th, 2015

The winery where we are meeting Dean and Patricia is in Temecula, CA. The area has exploded with wineries as the cities around it have had a huge housing boom. It seems that every time we come out, there is another new housing development catering to people looking to escape the housing prices in Los Angeles. What's crazy is many of these people commute about 100 miles each way into the city for work. The wineries have also had a huge boom. They have become popular destinations for the locals looking to have some fun on the weekends without the long drive back into the city.

It's 11 a.m. and we're right on time as we drive up to the winery. Dean and Patricia's motorhome is parked on the back end of the parking lot in a small dirt field adjacent to the vineyard. The lot is on top of a hill and the motorhome is positioned perfectly to maximize the view of the vineyard that runs into the valley below. Dean and Patricia are sitting outside, facing the vineyard working on their computers.

"Hey guys!" Patricia says as she gets up from her chair and comes over to greet us. "Dean is finishing up some work and then he's done for the day."

A minute later, Dean takes his headphones off and comes over to join us. We make introductions and they grab two extra chairs so we can sit and join them. The first thing that strikes me about these two is how relaxed they look. They remind me of a retired couple who have long since given up the stresses of work and all of the other daily bullshit. "Would you guys care for a glass of wine?" Dean asks with a smile as he heads into the motorhome.

I've read quite a bit about Dean and Patricia on their blog and feel like I already know them. They work for an online retailer that gives employees the ability to work from anywhere in the world. Dean and Patricia decided to give up the conventional life over three years ago and when they struck out on the road, these jobs fell into their laps. They weren't planning on working, at least not right away, but the opportunity was too good to pass up. They are able to set their own hours, preferring to work in the evenings and on weekends so they can sightsee during the week when they don't have to deal with the crowds.

"So Patricia tells me you two are planning to hit the road full time in a couple months?" Dean asks as he comes out with four plastic cups and a bottle of white wine. "Sorry about the plastic, but glass isn't too RV friendly."

"We completely understand," Kait says. "Yes, Patricia is right. We're hoping to leave sometime in May or June. Joe has an obligation with work and once that's complete, we'll be hitting the road."

"How exciting," Patricia says. "So have you bought an RV yet?"

"No, not yet," I respond. "We've been doing a lot of shopping, but we haven't found the one."

"What are you looking for?" She asks.

"We've been looking at used 38 to 42-foot diesel pushers. We have two big dogs and I don't think we'd want to go any smaller than that."

Dean and Patricia both look at each other for a second and Dean is the first to speak. "Have you guys ever RVed before?"

"No," Kait responds. "I used to do a lot of tent camping, but that's about it."

"Well if you don't mind me giving you some advice, you may not be too happy with something that big," Dean tells us. "Our rig is just over 25 feet long and we can get in almost everywhere. There are a lot of campgrounds that can't accommodate the larger RVs, plus it makes it a lot harder to boondock."

"Is yours gas?" Kait asks.

"Yep, it's gas," Patricia responds. "We read all those things online about how bad gas motorhomes are but when we saw this, we fell in love. It tows our Honda CRV fine. We might not be the fastest over the mountain, but we make it."

"Is it pretty noisy with the engine up front?"

"It's not too bad actually. It can get loud if you're going up a steep grade, but most of the time we're on flat roads and we have no problems. Do you guys want to go inside and take a look?"

"We'd love to," Kait and I say at the same time.

We follow Patricia into the motorhome and she gives us a quick tour. The motorhome is small, but it feels very comfortable, especially because it looks lived in. It can be hard to imagine what an empty motorhome will be like with all of our stuff, but now that I can see it, the whole thing feels much more real to me. Maybe we don't need all of that extra space?

Kait is asking Patricia about all the personal touches they put on the motorhome and I step outside to join Dean. "So you really have no issues with the gas engine?" I ask him.

"No, and I was one of those people who thought we had to get a diesel. The Ford V-10 engine is great and these gas motorhomes are a lot less expensive to maintain."

Dean starts giving me a tour of the storage bays because I tell him I'm concerned about not being able to bring all of my stuff, especially my tools. "Well, you're going to have to leave some of it behind, but I was able to bring the tools I wanted including a lot of crap we never use. Trust me, you won't use half the stuff you bring."

The ladies come back outside and tell us that they have decided we're all going to have lunch at the winery. The restaurant is packed with the weekend crowd, but we manage to get a table right away. Kait and I continue to pepper them with questions and they do their best to keep up.

"I'm so inspired by your motorhome," Kait tells Dean and Patricia as we're finishing the last bit of our lunch. Kait looks at me and says, "Honey, I think we can go small." Looking back I see smiles on Dean and Patricia's faces. "Okay, let's start looking more seriously at them."

After lunch, we head back to the motorhome and continue talking about what it's like to live out of an RV. As real as this adventure is becoming for me, I can't visualize how it might end. Sure, Kait and I told ourselves that we'd find jobs once the year was over, but that has been the extent of our planning. I wonder if we will want to stop after a year, or if we will find a way to keep this life going.

Around dusk, the mosquitos start to come out. Kait is allergic so we decide to say our goodbyes with the hope that we'll all meet again on the road. Driving home, Kait can't stop talking about our time with Dean and Patricia. After meeting them and seeing their motorhome, everything seems real rather than some fantasy we've been having. Many questions about whether this life is for us have been answered and we're ready to get back to motorhome shopping - smaller motorhomes that is.

10. GOING SMALL

"I'm feeling so inspired," Kait says. "Can't wait to shop for smaller motorhomes."

"I was surprised to see how much room they had," I say looking back at her. "Do we need all the extra space?"

"No. Think of all the places we can go with a smaller motorhome. I can't wait to camp at a vineyard. How amazing was that?"

"It was beautiful out there, plus what's better than having a few glasses of wine and walking back to your home which happens to be parked right next to the vineyard. It's too bad we had to leave," I say.

The two-hour drive home seems to fly by. We can't stop talking about small motorhomes and Kait was busy on her phone looking at all the different places we'll be able to go. It turns out, the national and state parks around the country have size limits for RVs. According to what Kait has found, the limit varies from park to park. While some don't measure, others have lines painted on the ground to keep people honest about how big their rig really is. It seems that having a motorhome 30 feet or shorter will allow us to get into most campgrounds. There are a few park campgrounds that limit anything larger than a van. If that's the case, we can always camp outside of the park and drive in with the Jeep to explore.

On our way home, we stop by the store to pick up a ribeye steak for dinner and fetch the boys from my mom's house. Duke and Leo are always excited when we drop them off and equally as excited when we pick them up. "Hey Joe, how was the meet up with your friends?" My mother asks. We tell her all about Dean and Patricia's small motorhome and how they were camped on a vineyard. "Wow that sounds incredible, but do you think you could live in something that small?"

"I think we could," I tell her. "There wasn't nearly as much room as the bigger motorhomes but the space was very well used. I don't think we'll need all that extra room, plus we can always go outside to extend our living area."

Back at the house, I get the grill fired up while Kait is sautéing some vegetables for our late dinner. As I am waiting for the grill to come to temperature, the back door slides open and Duke comes running out. "He wanted to come hang out with dad," Kait says with a smile.

"Where's Leo?" I ask.

"Oh, he's in the kitchen with me hoping I'll drop something."

After a fantastic dinner, Kait and I decide to spend the rest of the evening talking about small motorhomes and researching the different models.

"Is there anything we can tow with our Jeep?"

"I'm not sure. We have a 3,500 pound tow capacity and I don't know how big of a trailer we could tow."

Kait's question sets us off on a different path and we spend the rest of the evening looking for lightweight trailers. When we bought the Jeep we weren't worried about tow capacity because we weren't planning on towing anything with it. The number of trailers that we could potentially live in and tow with the Jeep is very limited.

"What about this one?" Kait asks turning her laptop to face me. She has the Lance 1575 pulled up on her screen. Fully loaded, the 1575 would push the limit of what our Jeep could tow, but if we don't fill it with stuff, then it might work for us. This is one of the few trailers in this size that has a full bath, queen size bed and a slide out for more room.

"Are there any dealers around that have one?" I ask her.

"There is a dealer not too far from us. They also have some gas Class A and C motorhomes. You want to go down there tomorrow?"

"Sure, I'd love to go."

Looking at pictures of the 1575, I can see the two boys and us living in something this small. Depending on options, MSRP is around $25,000. We could save a lot of money buying something like this and be able to travel longer with the savings.

We stayed up late last night looking at small trailers so we both slept in this morning. After a big breakfast and a long walk with the boys, we drive over to the RV dealership. When we arrive on the lot, there are quite a few trailers, larger motorhomes and even a decent selection of used units.

"How can I help you?" I hear as we are getting out of the Jeep.

"We saw online that you have a few Lance 1575 trailers and want to take a look at them," I respond.

"No problem, they're right over here. I'm Reggie," he says extending his hand to Kait and me.

We follow Reggie across the lot to the row of trailers. I immediately recognize the 1575 since it is much smaller than the other trailers on the lot. "Why don't you folks take a look through the trailer while I go and get a power cord to plug the trailer into so you can turn on all the lights and whatnot," Reggie says holding the door open for us.

For such a small trailer, the interior is spacious. To the right of the entry is a full size queen bed. It would require us to sleep East/West, which means Kait would have to crawl over me to get out of bed in the middle of the night. There are three windows around the bed that let in a lot of light and seem like they would provide great ventilation. Each window has a built-in screen and black out shade. Right above the bed is a small 12-volt TV and to the left is the kitchen area and a small closet. There's a three-burner gas stove and a decent size propane fridge on the opposite side.

From our research, a propane fridge seems to be the best option for us. We plan on doing as much boondocking (free off-grid camping) as we can and the residential style refrigerators use a lot of electricity. That would require us to either install solar and a big battery bank, or we would need to run the generator more. The propane fridge, on the other hand, runs off a small amount of propane and electricity allowing us to go a lot longer without having to charge the house batteries. The downside of a propane fridge is that they tend to be smaller, require more maintenance and the older models had problems with catching on fire. Considering manufacturers seem to have addressed most of the safety concerns with the new models, the benefits outweigh the disadvantages.

The rear of the trailer has a large wrap around dinette allowing four to five people to sit comfortably. The dinette is built into the slide, which is currently retracted, blocking access to the bathroom. This would be difficult if we parked at a place like Walmart for the night and we aren't able to put the slide out and need to use the bathroom.

The trailer starts making beeping sounds and I turn to see Reggie walking around to the entrance. "Okay, all plugged in. Let me put the slide out so you can get a better feel for the trailer." Reggie hits a button on the control panel and we hear the electric motor cranking for the slide. It takes about thirty seconds for the slide to extend out completely. Once it's out, the trailer feels like it has doubled in size.

"So are you folks planning on towing this with that Jeep of yours?" Reggie asks.

"That's the plan," I respond.

"We have a few customers who tow these with their Jeeps and have said they have no issues. They use them to camp out in the desert and then take the Jeep out on the trails."

"So kind of like a basecamp," Kait says.

"Exactly, let me show you some of the features of this trailer."

Reggie describes the main features and systems on the trailer and shows us how things work. Outside, Reggie opens the storage bay, which is a large pass through compartment that goes from one side to the other. The bay is not very tall, but it's long enough to fit quite a bit of stuff. There are also some cabinets inside the trailer for storage in addition to the small closet. Even with the storage, I don't know how we would fit all of our stuff, especially our clothes.

"Reggie, can we have a bit of time to hang out in the trailer and get a feel for it?" Kait asks.

"Sure, no problem. I'll go back to the office and come get me when you're done."

Once Reggie leaves, Kait looks over and asks, "So, what do you think?"

"It's nice for a small trailer, but I am not sure it would work for us. I feel like it would be tough with the two of us and the boys. There also isn't too much storage considering we will need supplies to live in here full time. We can use the

Jeep to store some things and maybe get a roof rack for more storage."

"I agree. I don't think we could live in something this small with Duke and Leo."

"At least we know that something like this won't work for us. I find it amazing how different photos online look compared to seeing the real thing in person. Do you want to check out some of the motorhomes they have?"

"Sure, why not."

When we get back to the sales office, Reggie comes out to meet us. "So what did you guys think?"

"It's nice, but I think it's too small for us and our dogs," Kait responds.

Reggie thinks for a minute before responding. "I don't think I have anything bigger that you could tow with the Jeep. That trailer is going to be about as big as you can go. Are you set on getting a trailer or would you be interested in looking at a motorhome?"

"We are. That's what we initially planned to buy. We got the Jeep as our toad, but we thought we might be able to go small with a trailer instead," I say.

"What are you planning to do with the motorhome?" Reggie asks.

"We are going to be full timing in it," Kait responds. "So this is going to be our home for at least the next year and we have two big dogs. If we get a motorhome, we'd like to try and keep it under 30 feet."

"Oh very cool. Do you two have jobs that will allow you to work on the road?"

"No, but we're saving to be able to do this for a year and then see how we feel about it."

"I keep telling my wife we'll do that someday. I have this 26-foot Class A gas motorhome if you'd like to see that?" Reggie says pointing to the motorhome parked right along the sales office.

Kait and I walk over to the small Class A and start examining the exterior of it. "This looks a lot like the motorhome Dean and Patricia have," she says to me.

"You're right, but this is a Fleetwood Flair."

Reggie returns with the keys and opens the Flair for us. The motorhome is mid-entry and as we walk in we notice the layout is very similar to Dean and Patricia's motorhome. Although the Flair is small, we've seen how useable the space can be and it doesn't seem that small now. Across from the entrance on the driver's side, is a small dinette that might fit four adults and a propane fridge to the left of it. The captain's chairs up front are turned around and there is a freestanding recliner on the passenger side. The kitchen is tiny with an L-shaped counter that has a three-burner gas stove on one side and a small sink on the other. The only counter space is in the back corner. There are covers for the stove and sink that provide more counter space when they're not in use.

In the back of the Flair, there is a walk around queen size bed and plenty of cabinets for storage. A section of the cabinets is on a small slide out that allows for a larger storage area and provides more room to walk by the bed. The nice thing is, we can still use the bed with the slide in.

After looking through the motorhome, I take a seat at the dinette. It feels small and not something I would be very comfortable sitting at for longer than a quick meal. The TV is above the driver's compartment and since there is no couch, the only good place to watch TV is to sit on one side of the dinette facing the TV or pull the recliner out into the middle of the living room.

"Can we take it out for a drive?" Kait asks Reggie.

"Sure, let me bring all the slides in and make sure the bay doors are closed."

Once Reggie is down the stairs I look at Kait and ask what she thinks.

"I like it. It's small, but I think this could work for us. What about you?"

Still sitting at the dinette I say, "It's okay. Sitting here is really not comfortable for me, but I'm curious to see how this drives compared to the diesels."

Once Reggie is done bringing the slides in, he pulls the motorhome out of its space to the front of the lot so I can take over. I hop in the driver's seat and get everything adjusted. The 26-foot Flair feels much smaller compared to the 42-foot Allegro Bus. The driver's seat is very basic and doesn't offer the support the seat in the Tiffin did.

Out on the road, the Flair is easy to drive and seems to have enough power. Reggie directs me to a hill so I can get a better sense of the engine noise in the cabin. Going uphill, the engine is loud, but not overwhelming. This is something I could certainly live with considering we'll be parked at a campsite more than we'll be driving. The ride is noticeably rougher than the Tiffin, but it's not a deal breaker. Pulling onto a large street with lots of traffic, I have no trouble making a tight right turn and switching lanes.

On the way back to the dealership, I feel a distinct pain in my lower back. I've had lower back issues for years and it flairs up, no pun intended, when I'm not in a seat with the right support.

"So what'd you think?" Reggie asks as we pull back into the lot.

"It's not going to work for us. Something with the seat is causing my back to hurt and there's no way I could drive this without taking pain meds. I did like the way it drove and found it much easier to maneuver than the last motorhome we took out."

Reggie doesn't seem too surprised. "Well the Flair is more of a budget conscious model and that seat doesn't have the same support many of the higher end units do. Have you checked out the Fleetwood Southwind yet?"

"No we haven't, I don't think I've even seen it online."

I'm not sure how we missed it in our research, but Kait and I both really like the Southwind Reggie shows us. At 34 feet, this motorhome is longer than what we're looking for, but it seems to be a great compromise between a high dollar diesel and a budget friendly gas motorhome. The front area of the Southward has a dinette and two flip around captain's chairs that look noticeably more plush and comfortable than the ones in the Flair. The dinette is across from the kitchen which has a decent size countertop, three-burner gas stove and a large double door propane fridge. My favorite feature of the Southwind is the L-shaped couch that I really like. The couch doesn't look as big, but it's comfortable to sit on with a 40-inch flat screen TV directly across from it. Below the TV is a faux fireplace.

The toilet and shower are behind the same door rather than separate doors with a hallway in between. I can see the advantages of both layouts, but I prefer having everything behind one door. There is a queen size bed and plenty of cabinets for storage. In fact, there are cabinets all over the motorhome and it seems like there is more than enough room for our stuff.

Although I found the Flair easy to drive, the driver's seat was a deal breaker. The Southwind has a comfortable front seat and I didn't have any issues with my back when we took it for a test-drive. The extra weight of the 34-foot Southwind and larger tires provide a smoother ride and is still easy to drive. After the test-drive, Reggie gives us some time alone.

"I really like this," I say to Kait.

"Me too, but it's a bit expensive. I wonder how much we can negotiate off MSRP?"

"I don't know. I can see us living in here. It's not as small as we want, but it does have many of the features we've been looking for in a motorhome. Plus, it drove much better than the Flair."

"I'm not ready to buy today, but let's go talk to Reggie and see if we can get an idea of pricing."

We find Reggie in his office and take a seat. "So is the Southwind more of what you're looking for?" He asks.

"It is, but we want to do a bit of research on it before we make a decision. Can we get an idea of your pricing on it?" I ask Reggie.

"Well MSRP on that particular motorhome with options is just over $153,000. I'd have to talk to our sales manager, but we could probably knock about $15,000 or so off of that. We also offer financing and can get you a good rate depending on your credit. Whenever you're ready let us know and we'll work with you."

We thanked Reggie for his time and headed home. "How much do you think we can get off the MSRP?" Kait asks once we're on the road.

"From what I've been reading we should be able to negotiate 20-30% off the MSRP. Reggie was willing to knock 10% off without even blinking an eye so there is definitely more room there. I'll do some research this week and see if I can reach out to other dealers and find out what their pricing is, but I think we found our motorhome."

"I do too. Let's see if we can find any used ones for sale."

"Good idea, I'm sure there are some that are a year or two old that we can get a great deal on."

11. WATER DAMAGE

Monday, April 27th, 2015

I have been spending most of my free time at work this week trying to find used Southwinds and reading up on what to look out for when buying used, especially water damage. Some people use RV inspectors with varying degrees of success, but I figure I can do all the inspection work myself. I have a lot of experience as a handyman as well as being a shade tree mechanic. I am the guy my friends call when they need help fixing something. Although I don't have any experience with a motorhome, everything is pretty straightforward as long as I know what to look for.

The used RV market is huge and many are sold through private sellers. As I'm looking for used Southwinds, I also find a few more options that could be a good match for us. I've contacted a handful of private sellers and keep running into the same problem. The seller either isn't responsive or they have a strange story about why they want to sell the motorhome. One guy told me he can't show the motorhome until the family was back in town because they still weren't sure if they want to sell. Then there are the people who have their used motorhome listed for more than what they cost new.

It's common knowledge that motorhomes take a big hit in value once they're driven off the lot. There's no way a sane person would pay more for a used motorhome when they can pick out a brand new one for less, and that's before negotiations. The most frustrating part of the used motorhome search is that it is nearly impossible to find the exact motorhome we want. When I do find one, it's located on the other side of the country. Now I can see why some people choose to only buy new. There's no doubt we have to take a big hit on the depreciation of a new motorhome, but we're able to walk onto a lot and pick out the make, model, floor plan and options we want. In some cases, we can even special order the motorhome directly from the manufacturer.

I feel my phone vibrate and look down to see a text from Kait, "Look what I found." I click on the link and see the exact Southwind we've been looking for. It's only a year old with a little over 6K miles at a great price.

I text back, "That's perfect. Let's go check it out this weekend before it gets sold."

"Sure and it's close to my parents' house. Maybe we can spend the night there?"

"I'm good with that, let me check with my mom to make sure she can take the dogs."

"Okay, I'm really excited!"

Although the week seemed to creep by, it's finally Saturday and we're on our way to the dealership. Kait called before we got on the road to make sure the Southwind was still there. They confirmed it was and the receptionist told her to ask for Bob. When we arrive at the sales office, Kait goes to find Bob while I look around the lot. The dealership is one of the biggest we've been to in California.

I see Kait walk out of the sales office with a salesman following her and she does not look happy. "The Southwind is sold even though they told me two hours ago when I called that it was still here," she says with Bob in tow.

"Sorry guys," Bob says. "Our Internet group hasn't updated the inventory on the site but I have some other units I can show you."

My stomach drops and I get the feeling that whomever Kait spoke to knew the motorhome was sold, but had us come down anyway.

"What do you think, hon?" I ask Kait.

"We drove all the way out here so we might as well see what else they have," she responds.

"Are you only looking for gas motorhomes or are you interested in seeing some diesels?" Bob asks.

"We'd prefer a gas motorhome, but we'd look at a diesel if you have any used under 35 feet," I tell him.

"I have a couple gas and diesel motorhomes I can show you; let's take a walk."

Bob shows us a couple motorhomes and we pass on them pretty quickly. The paint on the first one is starting to delaminate across the top edges of the body and looks like it has sat in the sun the last few years. The second unit smells like a mix of smoke and mildew. The third motorhome we see is a Newmar Ventana. From the outside it looks to be in great shape. "This is a 34-foot diesel pusher, same length as the Southwind, but the interior in this is going to be much nicer," Bob says as he unlocks the door.

The Ventana is three years old. The interior looks lightly used, which is confirmed when Bob tells me it has just shy of 10K miles. Kait and I spend a few minutes going through it and we like what we see, but the $179,000 asking price is way over our budget. Bob shows us a couple other units, but we don't see anything else we like.

"Can we go back and see the Newmar again?" Kait asks. "That's the only one I liked."

I don't say this in front of Bob, but I haven't been able to stop thinking about that Newmar. I thought the interior was a lot nicer than the Southwind and the layout felt more open. I don't know much about Newmar, but if we can get the price closer to our budget, we might be driving out of here with a motorhome.

Back at the Ventana, I ask Bob if he can leave us alone for a while so we can go through and check it out. "Not a problem," he says. "Just come get me when you're done."

We spend the next fifteen minutes going through the Ventana and the more we see, the more we like it. Not only is it comfortable, but Newmar's build quality seems to be better than other manufacturers we've seen. I brought along a flashlight so I could inspect the area behind the couch, inside of the cabinets and other nooks and crannies checking for the tale tell signs of water leaks or damage.

"Hey, Bob is walking back over," Kait says.

I'm about half way through my inspection of the bedroom and shake my head. "I guess he got tired of waiting for us."

"So what do you think?" Bob asks as he comes up the stairs.

"It's nice, but we'd like to go over it top to bottom and see if there are any issues," I tell him.

"No problem, but my sales manager just told me that if you two are interested in this motorhome, we could drop the price down to $110,000. He's going to be taking off in about thirty minutes and I can't do that deal without him."

I see red flags. Not only have they significantly dropped the price without us asking, but they're rushing us to make a decision. We've looked at a lot of motorhomes and that price seems to be too good to be true. Something is wrong.

"Wow, that's quite the price drop Bob," I say.

"I told my manager the two of you were a young couple looking to live out of a motorhome and tried to see what I could do for you. Trust me, this is a take it or leave it price and I doubt this unit will sit on the lot for more than a few days."

I've never been a big fan of salespeople and we seem to have met some very interesting characters while we've been shopping. We've heard all sorts of things to try and get us to buy, including misinformation. One salesman tried to convince me that the tow capacity of a motorhome was 5,000 pounds rather than the 3,000 I read on the manufacturer's website. When I told him the source of my information he tried to convince me that he has customers towing 4,500 pound Jeeps and it's not a problem. I've learned that most will say almost anything to make a sale, but Bob and his "sales manager" are working hard to take top spot as the sleaziest salesmen we've met so far.

Bob is right about one thing. This is a great deal at $110,000, but something doesn't seem right. I don't know if we'll walk into that sales office and have the manager tell us that the price is $160,000 and Bob just misunderstood him, but I am going to finish inspecting this thing first.

"Before we sit down with your sales manager, I need to go through this and check it out. We'll be staying in the area tonight and I'm sure your manager will be back in tomorrow."

Bob doesn't seem too happy and I don't care. I finish looking through the inside of the motorhome and find a cabinet door that's come off the hinges and a few other minor issues. "Don't worry about those," Bob tells me. "We can take care of them before you take delivery. Ready to go inside?"

"Not yet, I still need to inspect the outside," I tell him with some annoyance in my voice hoping he'll get the message to leave me alone.

The three of us go outside and I start walking around the exterior of the Ventana. There are some minor scratches but nothing too bad and the paint looks to be in great shape otherwise. The tires look good too and according to the date stamp, they are about four years old.

"Hey Bob, is it okay if I go up on the roof?" I ask.

Bob shrugs and then looks at Kait. "Is he always like this? I guarantee you this motorhome is in perfect condition. We inspect all of the used units before they go up for sale and we can sell you an extended warranty to cover any issues."

Kait scrunches her face at Bob and asks, "Perfect? What about the broken cabinet door inside the motorhome?"

That's my girl! I don't hear Bob's response because I am working my way up the ladder and need to pay attention. This motorhome is about thirteen feet tall and that would be a long fall. It doesn't seem like the previous owner maintained the seals around the roof. Although I see a lot of cracking, I didn't see any sign of leaking inside, but that doesn't mean water didn't make it in. I'll have to remember this as an issue that will need to be addressed. Otherwise everything looks fine on the roof.

Back down from the roof, I grab my flashlight and pop the rear cover of the engine. All of my experience has been with rebuilding and maintaining gas engines. I know very little about diesels, but this one looks pretty clean and I don't see any obvious issues. Depending on what this sounds like when we get it running, I may need to hire a professional to inspect the engine. Closing up the engine cover, I crawl under the motorhome with the flashlight to look for signs of rust, cracks and any damage from the previous owner driving over something they shouldn't have. I can see a bit of surface rust on some of the bolts and suspension components, but it doesn't look like there is anything to be concerned about. The airbags for the suspension look good and I don't see any cracks in the rubber. So far everything looks good. I wonder if there will be any issues once we drive it?

"Well, everything looks good," I tell Kait. I don't know what Bob has been saying to her, but she seems to be trying to keep a certain amount of distance between them.

"Did you check the bays?" Kait asks before Bob can try to push us back into the office.

"I completely forgot, let's pop the doors open and take a look."

"I don't think you'll find anything in there, they are completely empty," Bob says anxious to get this over with.

Shining my light into one of the bays, I see something that shouldn't be there. Looking through the rest of the bays I notice the same thing. It's hard to tell how serious this issue is by standing outside so I crawl into one of the pass through bays and notice the issue continues through the entire bay. I check the next bay and notice the same thing. "I think we have a problem here," I say.

"Problem? What kind of problem?" Bob asks.

"Look," I say pointing at the carpet lining the bay. "See that line? That's a water line. I know, because all of the screws up to this point are rusted and," I pull back a corner of the carpeting, "you can see some mold here. Every bay is like this. I don't know if this motorhome was in a flood or whether there was a leak inside that made it into the bays, but this is not good."

Bob shakes his head and puts on his sleaziest smile, "That's completely normal for a used motorhome. Nothing to worry about."

My blood pressure is now up and I look at Bob and ask, "Sorry, but are you trying to tell me that rust, water damage and mold is normal?" He hesitates for a moment so I continue, "You've got to be kidding me. Water damage isn't normal in a motorhome. Best case, all of the carpet in there needs to be torn out and replaced. More likely, wherever that water came from it also got into the walls and floors which means much bigger problems." I turn to Kait and say, "Let's go."

Bob starts walking out with us and we are trying to stay ahead of him. We walk straight past the sales office to the Jeep and Bob yells out, "Hold on, let me grab my card in case you see anything else you want to take a look at."

"Don't bother," I say over my shoulder as I open the door for Kait.

"What a sleaze ball! We're never coming back here again!" Kait says once I get into the Jeep.

"That guy was a real piece of work. I knew something was up when they dropped the price so quickly without us even asking. I'm starting to dislike RV salesmen."

"Me too. Let's head over to my parents' place."

Once I get on the freeway, Kait and I continue to vent about Bob and what happened at the dealership. "You know, I am starting to have doubts about buying used," I tell Kait. "All the used motorhomes we've seen have problems. It feels like we are buying a house that comes with the original furniture from the previous owners."

"I feel the same way," she says. "If we had enough time and money, we could buy something used and re-do the interior."

"Exactly. Plus who knows what problems we might find with it. I know they have extended warranties, but I've read a lot of bad things about them."

"So do you want to stop looking at used motorhomes and focus on new ones?" Kait asks.

"I think so. If we're going to be living in it, I would like to have new furniture and know we have a warranty through the manufacturer. Most of them are only one year, but we're only planning on doing this for a year and if we want to continue, we can look at getting an extended warranty then."

"Good point honey. I'm on board. No more used motorhomes."

12. EVERYTHING MUST GO

Saturday, May 2nd, 2015

"So we're in agreement that we are only going to look for new motorhomes, correct?" I ask Kait.

"That's correct."

"Okay, if that's the case, I feel like we pretty much have it narrowed down to the Southwind, but I don't want to buy anything until we have a better idea of when the merger will go through."

"We need to start thinking about listing the house," Kait says. "It's going to take us a while to get the yard in order and take care of any cosmetic issues. I think we should call John and have him come over, take a look at everything and give us an idea of how much work we need to do. I'd also like to know how long we should plan for the house to be on the market before it sells."

"You know, I've been so focused on finding a motorhome that I completely forgot about selling the house. It's already May and we're going to have a lot of work to do. I'll give John a call tomorrow and see if he can come by this week to look at the house."

John is booked most of the week, but he's going to make time to stop by on Wednesday. John helped us buy the house five years ago and we've stayed in touch with him and his family. Since we had a great experience with him the first time we wanted to work with him again to sell the house.

"I think John just pulled up," I yell into the bedroom. Duke is at the front door barking his head off and Kait can barely make out what I say over his roar. Leo is passed out on his bed and could care less that someone is here. Kait and I always joke that if burglars came into the house, Leo would either sleep through the whole thing or guide them to all the good stuff and demand a treat afterwards. He's a great dog, but there's not an ounce of protection in him.

"Hey Duke!" John says as he walks up the front steps. Of course he says hello to Duke first, everyone does. Duke has always been very standoffish when it comes to strangers and it takes him quite a few meetings before he warms up to someone. Once he does warm up, people seem to feel a sense of accomplishment and can't wait to see him again. Duke realizes it's John and runs over to lean up against his legs for some loving.

"Hey John, how's the family?" I ask as he comes in the door.

"Not too bad, everyone is doing well. I'm sorry to hear you'll be leaving us on this adventure, but it sounds like a fantastic idea. I've done some long road trips but never anything like what you have planned."

We catch up for a while and Kait comes into the living room after she's done changing. "Why don't we take a walk through the house and yard to see what we're going to have to do before we put this on the market," John suggests.

"Sounds like a plan," Kait and I say in unison.

"Jinx!" Kait says as she smiles at me.

We spend about twenty minutes going through the house, the backyard and the garage. John points out a couple issues and after we finish, John and Kait head into the living room while I get coffee started. Duke has stayed by John's side during the whole tour, getting more love every time we stopped to look at something.

Walking back with my coffee, I ask John, "So, overall what do you think?"

"Overall, I think the house is in great shape. You two have done a good job keeping it up and there are only some minor cosmetic issues. The wood floors still look good, but the carpets are going to need to be replaced. In my opinion, leave the carpet as it and we can give the buyer a credit for new carpet if they ask for it. The biggest problem you're going to have is with the front and backyard. There are a lot of dead spots, weeds and overgrowth. I would suggest you get that taken care of. Putting money towards landscaping will get you the most return because it adds curb appeal and if someone drives by, you want them to want to come in."

"Good point. We stopped watering the yard because of the drought and the weeds have since taken over," I explain to John. "Do you think we need to put sod down or can we do one of those zero scape yards?"

When the drought hit hard about a year ago, the City of Los Angeles offered an incentive to replace grass with what they call "zero-scaping." It's typically gravel or some kind of AstroTurf. Quite a few companies have sprung up that will come and replace the grass for free in exchange for signing over the incentive. About a quarter of the houses in the neighborhood have switched over. They look great at first, but after a few months, weeds invade and it looks terrible.

"Zero-scaping is popular, but most buyers still want grass or at least they think they do when they see a house. Considering you want to have the house listed in about a month, I don't think there will be time to pull everything out, re-seed and grow the grass. I'd suggest you sod the entire front and backyard. Plan to pay around six to seven thousand dollars. Once you're ready, give me a call and we can get the property listed."

"Sounds good, thanks John. We'll start getting all these things taken care of and update you towards the end of May," Kait says.

As soon as John leaves, Kait turns to me and says, "I don't want to spend six or seven thousand on laying down sod. I don't think it's necessary. What do you think?"

"I don't know if we need to spend the money on sod, but I agree with John that the house needs curb appeal. Think about that first impression you get when you see a house for sale. If the yard is nice and manicured you have a much better feeling about it than if the grass is dead and full of weeds."

"I guess you're right, but can we try to do this ourselves?"

"It's going to take a lot of work and we're going to have the rest of the house to deal with on top of our full time jobs. Let me talk to my mom and find out who takes care of her yard and I'll call to see if he can help us. So what are we going to tackle first inside the house?" I ask Kait.

"We need to start getting rid of stuff. There are untouched boxes in the guest room closet from when we moved in. We can't paint or get the house cleaned until we empty out the rooms. I'm so excited to start getting rid of things! Let's have a garage sale this weekend."

"Okay, but I am putting you in charge of getting things ready for the sale."

Friday, May 8th, 2015

Our three-bedroom house is full of stuff that we've collected over the years. It's amazing how much we accumulated and Kait is on a mission to empty every closet. She's so excited that she invited her friend Marc, who apparently loves having garage sales, to come over and help. As ready as I am to lead a much more minimalist lifestyle, it's been hard to go through all of my stuff and get rid of things. We briefly talked about a storage unit, but it wasn't worth the cost and we don't have any desire to settle back in California once we're on the road.

Marc comes over around 6 p.m. and gets right to work with Kait. While they're inside, I head into our detached garage, which I've claimed as my own, to sort through everything and see what I can put out at the garage sale. The garage has always been a nice escape when I feel like working on something or just want to be by myself. Kait typically leaves me alone when I am in here, but Duke and Leo like to venture in every now and again to see what I am up to and to get a little bit of grease on their ears. Tonight, they are too interested in what's going on inside the house so I'm on my own. One of the things I'll miss the most about the house is this garage.

Sitting on my stool, I survey the little empire I've built. It's difficult to decide what's coming with us and what I have to get rid of. I have two, maybe three, full sets of tools that I've acquired over the years. About half of that was inherited when my father passed away. There are a couple jacks, stands and just about everything the home mechanic needs. There simply won't be room to bring everything so I need to put together one good set of tools that is small enough to go in the motorhome, but has everything I think I'll need. Most of what I inherited from my father are the old school Craftsman tools and those will make up the basis for the set of tools I am bringing. I can fill any gaps with the cheap "Made in China" tools that I picked up when I was starting out and sell everything else.

On my workbench, I have some power tools and a vise press that I won't have room for. Opposite the bench, I have five motorcycles to sell. Two of them are set up for racing, a highly modified Graves Yamaha R6 and a Kawasaki Ninja 250. I raced the R6 and I was hoping to get Kait on the 250 once she got her license, but it sat in the garage collecting dust. Two of the other bikes are old Honda cruisers I used to ride but need a lot of work. The last bike, a Suzuki SV650S is my daily driver. It's going to be hard to let her go. Since I'm selling all of my motorcycles, all of the race equipment can go too.

There is yard equipment scattered throughout the garage. The shelves are filled with random things that I have picked up over the years. I have to make sure I don't get rid of anything I will need when we start work on the house and yard. Then there are all the miscellaneous things that have mysteriously made their way in here like an ice cream maker. I have no idea where that came from. After a few productive hours, I head back in the house to see how Kait and Marc are doing.

"But what about this? Don't you think we'll need it?" My arguments seem to be falling on deaf ears. While I was in the garage, Kait and Marc have taken the liberty of going through most of my stuff and they've made piles in the living room of things for the garage sale. They have mountains of clothes, kitchenware and other odds and ends. Marc is putting price tags on everything, including the furniture. I had no idea we had this much stuff in the house, but half of it seems like things we should keep and take with us.

"How many times have we used that in the last year?" Kait asks referring to the cocktail shaker I am holding.

"Uh, once or twice I think." I can see where this is going.

"Okay, and are you going to use it on a regular basis when we're in the motorhome?"

Putting the shaker down I say, "No, probably not. You're right, but my parents gave this to us so it's hard to let it go."

"I know many of these things have sentimental value, but we can't take it all. If we haven't used it, we don't need it," Kait says and looks across the piles of things around the room.

"How much stuff do we have left?" I ask.

Marc looks up and says, "Go take a look in the office and guest room. We pulled almost everything out of the closets and drawers so we could get a better idea of how much there is and what needs to go."

In the office, the floor is covered with stuff. I can hardly find a place to step trying to walk in the room to get a good look at everything. The guest room is no different, except Marc was wrong about one thing. The closet is still full of boxes filled with Christmas decorations. I had no idea we had this much stuff and feel completely overwhelmed. Where did all of this come from?

When we moved in, we didn't even have furniture for the house and spent the first few months sitting on camping chairs in the living room. Now, we're buried in what we've collected over the years. Most of it sits on a shelf or in a box taking up room. We haven't used most of these things and I realize that all of this stuff is weighing us down. That weight will be lifted once we get rid of it all.

"Okay, I'm on board. Let's get rid of all of it," I tell Kait and Marc as I walk back into what was once our dining room.

In the morning, our driveway is lined with items for the garage sale. We were up past 2 a.m. last night getting everything ready and priced. Marc decided to spend the night and help us with the sale today.

As I am bringing out another load of decorations we no longer have a use for, a gentleman walks halfway up the driveway and asks, "Are you selling any tools?"

"I have quite a few I'm selling, want to take a look?"

"Yes, please. I'm going to be rebuilding my engine soon and need to pick up some tools."

I open the garage door and see his eyes go wide looking at all the tools I have laying out. "Go on in and take a look," I tell him.

He immediately walks over to the pile of tools I plan to keep and asks, "How much for these?"

"Sorry, those aren't for sale. I'm selling everything over there," I say pointing to the other piles on the ground. He looks disappointed, but moves over to the other side and starts going through the piles. I point out different tools that I bought when I rebuilt one of the motors on my motorcycles and show him the lifts and ramps I have for sale.

"Okay, I'll take everything, how much?" he asks.

I wasn't expecting that. I have a rough idea of what I want for everything so I tell him, "$800 for all of it."

He's shaking his head at this offer; "I'll go maybe...$300 for it."

I chuckle a bit at his offer. "No way. I can get more than that for these," I say pointing to the lifts and stands I am including in the sale.

We continue to go back and forth and in the end we pull out a few things he doesn't need and agree on $500 for the lot. Although I am sad to see them go, at least now I won't have to worry about people trying to nickel and dime me on every tool I have for sale.

"Hey babe, check this out!" I say holding up the five crisp hundred dollar bills. "Our first sale of the day. I just sold most of my tools."

"Wow, congratulations! How do you feel about that?" She asks.

"Well, I'm happy they're sold, but it's hard because those were all of my tools and I had a connection to them. I could care less about selling our duvet cover, but getting rid of my tools is tough."

The rest of the day goes well. We got quite a bit of traffic and sold most of what we had out. Kait packed up the left-over odds and ends in the Jeep and dropped them off at the Salvation Army. My motorcycles didn't sell, but I priced them a bit high. I guess I'm not quite ready to let go of them.

13. NEGOTIATIONS

Saturday, May 30th, 2015

It's been a couple of weeks since our meeting with John and my mother's landscaper is inspecting our yard. He says it will be a lot of work, but he can get the yard cleaned up, re-seeded and bring in some flowers to brighten it up. He doesn't seem to think that it will be a problem to have grass growing by late June and will maintain the yard until the house is sold. The best part is, the cost will be a fraction of what it would have been to put down sod. With the yard in good hands, we can focus on the house.

Kait and I need to paint some of the rooms, fix a few odds and ends, and repaint the outside of the house. We kept the cans of paint the previous owners used, all I need to do is have some more mixed up.

"We'll be ready to list the house at the end of June based on our progress," Kait says. "John said we should expect to be in escrow within thirty days of listing the house which means we could have the house sold by late July, early September depending on how escrow goes. Do you think the merger will go through by then?"

"Based on information I've gathered in the transition meetings, it should happen soon but you never know. I say we keep moving forward because it's completely out of our control. That does bring up something I've been meaning to talk to you about. I think we should buy the motorhome soon. Since we're going to finance, we need to have our jobs and house to get the best interest rate possible. Plus, it will make life much easier if we can move from the house into the motorhome. Otherwise, we might have to move everything into a storage unit, then move into the motorhome. We can also practice boondocking in the driveway and iron out the kinks."

"I don't know, there is a lot to think about with listing the house and the merger. What if the merger doesn't go through?"

"If that happens, I'm still leaving the company. The extra money from the retention bonus would be great, but we've managed to save more than enough and I've realized that I would rather enjoy my life than be stuck in a cubicle waiting for a check."

"You're right. We're going to have to buy the motorhome sooner or later and it might be better to do it now rather than when we're in the middle of selling the house."

"Then I will get the financing nailed down and if all goes well, maybe we can pick it up this weekend?"

"Are we set on the Fleetwood Southwind?" Kait asks.

"I thought we were. We both like it and I think the layout is perfect for us. I would prefer something smaller, but we haven't seen anything under 30 feet that we like. Are you having doubts about it?"

"No, I just want to make sure we are still on the same page. I would like to go take another look at the Southwind before we make a decision. We also don't know if they are willing to come down 20-30% on their price. If we can get a better deal in another state, I would be willing to fly out to buy the motorhome and drive it back."

"Good point. I've done some research on pricing but let me dig a bit more and see what I can come up with. I'll also find out what our financing options are," I tell Kait.

After a few days of researching financing options, I find what I think is the best deal. Costco has a finance program for their members and the rates are slightly better than others I've found. The odd thing is that they state they'll need to get financial records, tax returns and various other documents in order to verify us for the loan. I don't think we needed to provide this much information when we bought the house. After twenty minutes on the phone with a loan officer, our application is submitted. The representative told me that they will start the process with our credit and salary information and if they need anything else, we'll get an email with instructions on how to supply additional documents. The downside is the approval can take one to two weeks depending on how many applications they have to process. It's Wednesday and I doubt we'll be approved by this weekend, but at least we can go back and take another look at the Southwind to make sure it's what we want.

With financing tackled, it's time to figure out how much we should pay for the Southwind. My first stop is the RV Trader website. Most dealers have the Southwind listed at MSRP, but a few have it listed with huge discounts. From everything I've read, it's a known industry practice for the manufacturers to inflate the price of RVs so dealers have room to negotiate. At least now I know why all of the RVs at shows are "on sale." They're not on sale; they just have them priced to make the buyers feel like they are getting this big discount.

I found a dealer in Florida with a large inventory of Southwinds. I send them an email asking if they can give me their best price as I would like to have something in writing before booking a flight to Florida. Within an hour I receive a response.

Mr. Russo,

Hope all is well and would like to personally thank you for considering our dealership for all of your camping needs! We pride our self in customer service! Here is the information on the Southwind 34a. My store has 4 models in stock and those are all the same. So here is what we can do.

— —-

Breakdown:
MSRP: 153,363.00
DISCOUNT: 47,368.00
SALE PRICE: 105,995.00

PREP: 1,250.00
FREIGHT: 1,495.00
DOC FEE: 299.00
SALES TAX: 6,542.34
COUNTY TAX: 50.00
TAG/REGISTRATION: 450.00

——

FINAL BALANCE: 116,081.34

——

LET US HELP YOU SAVE ALMOST $50,000 ON A NEW FLEETWOOD!
THANK YOU AGAIN

That's 30% off MSRP and while I'd rather not fly to Florida and have to drive the motorhome all the way back to California, I will seriously consider it if we can't get a similar deal locally. I forward the email to Reggie and ask if they can match the price.

Hello Joe,
So that dealer is really selling you the southwind at $109,039 (price with prep, freight and doc fee)? Now remember that we do not take our units to shows, they are locked on our lot so people can only go into them when one of us are around. We know that dealer very well but keep in mind that

they are on the east coast so you are most likely going to have some rust issues and then the cost of getting up there and driving back needs to be accounted for, plus when you get back to California you have to register the unit here and also pay the difference in sales tax. Now with that being said what we can do for you on our unit on the lot would be as follows:

PRICE = $112,000
TAX = $10,087.20
DOC FEE = $80.00
DMV FILING FEE = $29.00
LICENSE FEE = $729.00
TRANSFER = $91.00
TIRE DISPOSSAL FEE = $10.50
TOTAL OUT THE DOOR = $123,026.70

You guys know us and should know that we are straight shooters here. You will have no surprises when purchasing from us. You will not have any DMV issues and will not have to pay out of pocket the difference in sales tax. You are financing so if purchased else where you are responsible for DMV fees as well as any difference in tax. Give me a call when you have some free time.

Thank You,
Reggie

Kait has already weighed in. She's been following the email threads and thinks staying local would be best for us and I agree. I've read new motorhomes can have all sorts of bugs to work out and it would be good to start a relationship with our local dealer to get those issues taken care of before we're on the road full time. Plus, after the Florida dealer's fees and the difference in California taxes and registration, there's only about a $2,000 difference in price over our local dealer. We'll probably spend more in airfare and gas to get the Southwind back here.

After we get home from work, we take the dogs for a long walk and talk about the email exchanges I had with the dealers today. As we turn to head back to the house, Kait asks, "How safe are motorhomes?"

"Huh, good question. I have no idea. I don't remember seeing airbags in any of the motorhomes we drove and they don't seem to have much protection up front, at least not in the Class A motorhomes. I'll do some research when we get home."

As much as I enjoy our regular walks around the neighborhood, I can't wait to show the boys the rest of the country. Another big reason we chose to live in a motorhome is to spend more time with Duke and Leo. We hate leaving them every day while we are at work. Duke is getting old and our guess is that he's around twelve and Leo is about eight or nine. We want to be able to spend as much time with them as possible.

As soon as we get home I start looking for the answer to Kait's question. My guess is that I'll have to dig through reports and all sorts of other data to come up with a solid answer. After a quick Google search I realize the answer is fairly straightforward. Aside from seat belts, there aren't any crash safety features on a Class A motorhome unless we get one built on a bus chassis like the Prevost. Some manufacturers claim they build a more solid structure or have steel beams up front to help protect passengers but in general, Class A motorhomes aren't crash tested and are built to have everything people need to live comfortably, not to survive a serious crash. It's scary to think that the only thing in front of us in a front-end collision is the windshield and a piece of fiberglass.

My next Google search is, "safest motorhome." I find a few videos and articles talking about how many of the Class C motorhomes are a much better option. These are built on a van chassis and while the "box" sitting on the back is not crash tested, the original manufacturer has tested the front cab. The safest of these are the Super Cs, built on a semi-truck chassis like Freightliner or Volvo and those chassis undergo rigorous crash testing. Plus, a big steel bumper and huge engine up front offers added protection. Some of the Class Cs even come with airbags.

"Looks like Class As aren't safe at all," I tell Kait. "No airbags. They aren't crash tested. Basically, we will be rolling the dice hoping we don't get in a serious accident."

"That's not good. Are there any motorhomes out there that are safer?"

I go through my research with her and explain that if we want something safe, we should check out a Super C. I'm already thinking about how cool it would be to drive a semi-truck around the country. Of course, there is a dealer near Kait's parents' house with a few Super C motorhomes for sale.

"Why don't we do this," I tell Kait. "On Saturday, let's go down to the dealer near your parents' house and see what we think. The problem is, even if we can get 30% off the MSRP, it's going to be about $50,000 more than the Southwind."

"True, but if it's safer and drives better, it might be worth considering."

I never expected that response from Kait, but I am certainly game to go check out a semi-truck based motorhome.

That Friday, I receive an email that our financing has been approved. I applied for $150,000 just in case - seems like I may not have been too far off if we like the Super C.

14. WE MAKE AN OFFER

Saturday, June 6th, 2015

"I've really enjoyed going motorhome shopping with you, but I'll be happy if this is the last time we drive two hours to a dealership," Kait says as we head out Saturday morning to go look at the Jayco Seneca. I've spent the last couple days researching the Seneca and it seems most owners love them. They have some quirks like a whistling noise from the side view mirror but nothing that can't be easily remedied. The problem is that there are fewer Jayco dealers compared to Fleetwood, so it has been more difficult to get an idea of how much they are selling for.

"I've enjoyed shopping with you too, but why do we always have to go when it's so hot?"

"I have no idea, but I think it's supposed to get above 100 today." Because of the heat, Kait's parents decided to sit this one out. Who can blame them? I'd rather be relaxing in air conditioning right now.

When we get to the Jayco dealership, the salesman takes us to see the Senecas on the lot. There are four lined up side by side. We already know that the 38FK is our favorite floor plan and ask to see that model. Learning from previous mistakes, due to being uninformed, I could probably recite the spec sheet and features on the FK from memory. At this point, we only need the salesman to unlock the door and let us do our thing since we know what we're looking for.

The Seneca looks a lot bigger in person than I expected. It's at least four feet longer than the Southwind and appears much sturdier. We had hoped to get something under 30 feet, but that may not be possible with the other requirements we have. Safety is a concern as well as the durability of the engine and chassis. I've also found through my research that Super Cs can be serviced at truck stops for a fraction of what RV dealerships charge.

The salesman opens up the FK for us and has no problem letting us go through the motorhome alone. Since it is 100 degrees out, the first thing I do is check to see if the motorhome is plugged into shore power so I can turn on the A/C. According to the thermometer, it's 90 degrees inside the motorhome. This will be a good test to see how quickly the A/C cools the rig.

"It's very roomy in here," Kait says.

One downside to most Class C motorhomes is that the front driver's cab area is not part of the living space. However, in this model the cab over bed and a large living room slide on the passenger side helps open the space up. The couch and dinette are built into the slide and on the opposite side is a large kitchen. Along one of the walls of the living room is a TV with a faux fireplace beneath it. The one problem I see with the location of the TV is it will be covered when the slide is in. Otherwise the living area is fully functional with the slides in. The bathroom is in a hallway that leads into the rear bedroom and is fairly roomy. In the bedroom, there is a lot of storage space with a walk around king size bed. The Southwind only has a queen size bed and considering we sleep in a king now, moving to a queen would be an adjustment.

"So what do you think?" I ask Kait.

"I really like it. Did you try the front seat yet to see if it's comfortable for you?"

After we test-drove the Flair and my back pain flared up, Kait has been very concerned about finding a motorhome that I am comfortable driving. She plans to drive as well, but doesn't want to be the only one behind the wheel.

"No I haven't, want to join me up front?"

"I'd love to."

We have to duck down to go from the living area into the cab. It's not difficult although I'm sure one of us will hit our head eventually. My money is on Kait doing it first. I like the driver and passenger doors up front because we can use those instead of having to crawl back and go out the side door.

"This seat is so comfortable," I tell Kait.

"So is mine. I like having the driver's compartment separated from the living area. This feels like a dedicated area for driving."

"Of course it does, we're sitting in the cab of a semi-truck. This is a stretched Freightliner M2 chassis, which is smaller than a lot of semis out there, but it's still meant to pull trailers around the country. Want to take it for a drive?"

"Of course and I want to drive today. You take it out first and then I'll drive us back," Kait says.

I find our salesman and he grabs the keys for the Seneca. Once he pulls it out of the dealership I jump in the driver's seat. "Can we drive to a quiet area so my wife can take over and try driving as well?" I ask.

"Absolutely, there's a commercial park not too far from here that is a ghost town on the weekends."

The Seneca is probably one of the easiest motorhomes I've driven so far. Although it has air ride suspension in the back, it's not as smooth as the Tiffin. The driving position with the hood and front wheels out in front makes it feel more natural - like I'm driving a car. In a Class A, the driver's seat is right above or just forward of the front wheels, which makes it feel like driving a bus. There isn't too much noise with the engine up front and quite a bit of power for something this big.

"Okay babe, your turn," I tell Kait once we reach the commercial park. Our salesman was right, there is no one around which is a good thing because Kait is going to have to make a U-turn to get us out of here. The salesman starts to get up from the passenger seat so I can sit with Kait, but before he does, I tell him he'd better stay where he is - this is Kait's first time driving a motorhome.

"Okay, I'm ready," she says.

The salesman shows her how to release the air brakes and explains the Jake brake. I've always heard them on big rigs but never knew what they did - it's a system that, when the driver lets up on the gas pedal, releases the pressure built up in the cylinders causing the truck to slow down, otherwise known as engine braking. Engine braking in diesel-powered vehicles doesn't normally occur unless a Jake brake system is installed. It's certainly a nice feature when driving something this large.

Although it's her first time behind the wheel, Kait has no problem making the U-turn and driving us back to the dealership. She even took the Seneca onto the freeway for a few exits and then through a residential neighborhood. When we pull back into the dealership lot, Kait has a grin that goes from ear to ear.

"So what did you two think?" The salesman asks.

"It was very easy to drive and I felt completely comfortable behind the wheel," Kait responds.

"Would you like to go inside and go over some numbers?"

"Give us a few minutes and we'll let you know," I tell him.

Once he's gone, I don't have to ask Kait if she likes it. We're both impressed with this motorhome, but it's big and well over our budget. Kait seems to be reading my mind, "Why don't we go tell him we need some time to think about it and go grab some coffee so we can talk this over," she says.

We find a coffee shop down the road and spot a TGI Friday's a few doors down when we pull up. "I don't know about you, but a beer and some wings sound good right now," I say to Kait.

"I'm starving. Let's go there instead and talk about the Seneca over a beer."

Halfway through my beer I tell Kait, "I like the Seneca and would like to make an offer on it."

"Are you sure? It's a lot bigger than what we want and the MSRP is $232,000." Pulling out her calculator, she looks up and says, "30% off that is a little over $162,000. Add in tax, fees and registration it will be more than the Southwind. Do you think it's worth the extra money?"

"Well it's bigger, a diesel, and built on a semi-truck chassis. It's going to be safer than the Southwind plus it was much more comfortable to drive. Do I think that is worth an extra $50,000? Sure, if those are things that matter to us."

"It's more than what we budgeted and I'm not comfortable going that high," Kait says. "I like it, but I'm only willing to pay $160,000 for it. I think that's a good price for the Seneca and if they're willing to accept that, I'm willing to buy it."

As I've learned, when the Price Terminator has a number, there's no budging. We agree to hold at that price and once we're finished with our beer and wings we head back to the dealership.

Walking into the lobby of the sales office, I tell our salesman, "We like the Seneca, but we need to discuss the price."

"Sure, come on back into my office and we can talk."

When we get into his office, he pulls out a pad of paper and his pricing sheets for the RVs on the lot. He studies the list for a moment and then writes the MSRP on the pad. Below that, he writes "$32,000" and subtracts that from the MSRP, circling the "$200,000" result. He turns the pad around and pushes it towards the two of us. We both smile at each other and then back at the salesman.

"Can I have your pen?" I ask. The salesman hands it over and I write down the number Kait and I agreed on and slide the pad back to him. Shock seems to be an understatement for what I can see on his face.

"Wow, okay. Let's cut the BS and just tell me what you're willing to pay for the Seneca so we can skip the back and forth," he says with a very expectant look.

"That's what we're willing to pay," I say pointing to the pad. "If you agree to that, we'll sign the papers and be on our way," I tell him.

"Okay," he says after another minute of contemplating. "So to be clear, if we accept this offer, you'll buy the Seneca right now?"

"Yes, that's correct."

The salesman scribbles on the pad again and hands it back to me with the pen. He's crossed out the previous numbers, circled the "$160,000" and added "Final offer, if accepted will purchase today."

Once Kait and I have a chance to look at the pad, he says, "I'm going to take this to my manager and I'd like you to sign next to what I wrote there so he knows you're serious. I don't know if we can get to that price, but at least by signing it he'll know how serious you are."

"Does that work for you?" I ask Kait.

"I don't see why not," she says.

I grab the pen and sign my name next to the offer. The salesman takes the pad and walks out of the office.

"I'm really nervous," I tell Kait. I realize I am shaking and sweating a bit because if they accept this offer, we'll be buying a motorhome today. What are we getting ourselves into? $160,000 is a LOT of money and I'm panicked that the salesman is going to come back in and say "Congratulations!"

"I can't believe they're actually considering the offer," Kait says. "I figured the sales guy would just laugh at us and say 'Thanks, but no thanks.' Now if they accept, we have to buy it. Did we do the right thing?"

"I don't know. I'm panicking a bit, but we both agreed that if we could get it at that price, it would be a good deal. I didn't think about the fact that we would actually be spending $160,000 until he walked out of the office with the sheet I signed."

A few tense minutes later the salesman walks back in and introduces us to his manager.

"I'm sorry, but we can't accept your offer. It's too low and we'd be losing money on this motorhome. The lowest I could go if you purchased today would be $165,000," the manager says to us.

"$160,000 is the highest we can go. This is more than what we budgeted and we don't want to add another five thousand to that."

"I'm sorry we can't go any lower than that. The reason it took me so long to get you an answer was because I called the owner to ask if he'd accept your offer. Again I'm sorry that we couldn't get together on this, but $165,000 is the absolute lowest I can go."

We thank both men and walk back to the Jeep. As much as I like the Seneca, a huge wave of relief has come over me and I'm happy they didn't accept the offer. It's a great motorhome, but the payment would have been much more than we planned and it would have eaten into our savings that much faster. Maybe beers and motorhome shopping isn't such a good idea.

15. FINDING THE ONE

On the long drive home, Kait and I talk about how relieved we both feel that the deal didn't work out on the Seneca.

"So do you think we should start looking for a used Seneca?" I ask Kait.

"For the price of a used Seneca we could buy a new Southwind, have the factory warranty and not inherit someone else's problem. I'm concerned about the lack of safety features, but I don't think it's worth the premium. I still like the Southwind and if I remember correctly, Reggie is going to be there tomorrow. We can go over, take another look and make sure we still like it. We should also ask if they could come down a bit more on the price. Their offer was good, but no reason not to see if there is a bit more room."

Back at home, Kait and I sit down on the couch and both instinctively open our laptops. Looking at motorhomes has become our hobby over the last year and the dogs love it because we can pet them while we scroll through listing after listing.

"Do you remember that motorhome we looked at with the water damage and sleazy salesman?" I ask Kait without looking up from my computer.

"Yeah, why?"

"Was that a Newmar? I can't remember."

"I'm not sure, but the model was a Ventana. Is that a Newmar?"

Checking Newmar's site, I confirm it is. Aside from the water issues, we liked the build quality and layout of the Ventana, but it's the only Newmar we've seen.

"I found a few Newmar dealerships in the area. Come over and check out the gas motorhomes they have."

Kait moves over next to me on the couch so she can see my screen as I scroll through this dealer's inventory. I click on the Bay Star 2903 and start looking at the pictures.

"Can you pull up pictures of the interior?" Kait asks.

I click on the interior images and start scrolling through each one.

"The 2903 is very nice," Kait says. "How long it is?"

"That's what you're not going to believe. It's 30 feet. Well, technically it's 29 feet and 11 inches."

"Hey, an inch is an inch," Kait says.

"That's what she said!" I say with a big grin.

"Oh boy," Kait says shaking her head. "I like it. It looks like it's a little less expensive than the Southwind. I'd like to take a look at this before we finalize things with the Southwind. The website says email for quote, can you send them a note? I'm curious to see what their price is on it."

"Sure, I'll email them right now."

About an hour later, I get an email back from a salesman at the dealership. "Hey babe, I already got an email back from the Newmar dealer. His price on the Bay Star is less than what they want for the Southwind. Should I tell him we'll come down on Saturday to take a look at it?"

"Wow that was fast. We can go in the morning and if we don't like it we can go buy the Southwind. Ohhh I'm so excited!"

The week is crawling by once again. I'm worried that the Newmar is going to be sold before we get to the dealer so I've been checking their website every day to make sure it's still there. I've also been busy reading up on Newmar and their models. I don't think I've found a single RV manufacturer that doesn't have issues, but the biggest difference is how each of the manufacturers deal with those issues. Some make customers jump through hoops to get any type of warranty work done. Others will take their sweet time sending parts or approving work orders. Newmar seems to be very good about dealing with issues head on. From what I've been reading, they will overnight parts, approve warranty requests within a day or two and send out mobile techs if we're not able to get into a dealership. There are also reports from many customers who say that the customer service reps will call to make sure warranty work is getting done to their expectations. From what I can tell, Newmar has great customer service and stands behind their product.

Saturday, June 13th, 2015

Last night, I probably got about three hours of sleep because I couldn't stop thinking about the Newmar. When I got up this morning, I emailed the salesman again to let him know we'd be in this morning and he confirmed that the Bay Star is still there. The 2903 is the exact size motorhome we've been looking for and from the photos, it looks great, but those rarely tell the whole story. If a picture is worth a thousand words, you'd need a million to accurately describe a motorhome. We've walked into some motorhomes that look great in the photos but are a total let down in person. It's amazing what a wide-angle lens and good lighting can do.

When we pull up to the dealership, I spot the Bay Star 2903 parked in front of a fleet of other Newmar motorhomes. From the looks of it, they also have a decent selection of other new and used motorhomes on the lot.

"Hey you guys, I'm Ron. You must be Joe and Kait."

"Yep, that's us," Kait says. "Nice to meet you, Ron."

"Great to meet you as well. I pulled the Bay Star around so you can go through it, why don't we go in and take a look."

When we walk inside, Ron has all the lights on, the TV going with the surround sound and he's dressed it up with table settings and other touches that make it feel homey. Of course the A/C is running because, as usual, it's already hot out and only getting hotter. The inside of the Bay Star is surprisingly big for something under 30 feet long. We both remark on this and Ron tells us that's because of the full wall slide that runs from behind the driver's seat to the end of the motorhome. There is also a second slide in the bedroom that provides even more space.

The front seats are turned around as part of the living area. Next to the driver's seat on the full wall slide is a pull-out couch with a queen size inflatable mattress strapped to the back. Across from the couch is a nice sized kitchen with good counter space, a double stainless steel sink, three-burner gas stove and a propane fridge. Next to the couch is a comfortable dinette that converts into a small bed. I doubt we'd ever use it as a bed, but it's a cool option. There are cabinets throughout the living room area with more than enough storage for our belongings. There is even a large floor to ceiling pantry with pull out shelves. The only thing I see that I don't like is the location of the living room TV. It's mounted above the captain's chairs so we'd have to look sideways while sitting on the couch to watch TV. That wouldn't be comfortable and my neck would not appreciate it.

Across from the pantry is the full bathroom, large enough for one person to use at a time. The shower is larger than some of the other units we've looked at. I can stand in it without hitting my head and wash without bumping the walls. The rear bedroom is quite roomy with both slides extended and there are more cabinets and drawers for storage. There is a small, full length closet and two half closets that are tall and deep enough to hang shirts and jackets. The bed is a walk around residential queen that can be lifted to reveal a storage area underneath. The TV in the bedroom faces the bed so it would be much more comfortable to watch in here than out in the living room. In fact, we only have one TV in our three-bedroom house. This small motorhome has not one but two TVs and the funny thing is, most other motorhomes we've seen have three or four TVs.

Ron walks us through the different features and additional options of the Bay Star. There are extra windows in the bedroom and kitchen, additional insulation in the roof and heating pads under the tanks to keep them from freezing during the winter. Ron is not the typical salesman and knows the Bay Star inside and out. He seems to enjoy what he's doing and it doesn't feel like he's trying to push anything on us.

"Can we see the motorhome with the slides in?" Kait asks.

"Absolutely, but I'm going to have you do it," Ron says as he opens a small cabinet above the entry to reveal the control panel.

"First, we need to make sure everything is out of the way. Joe, can you flip the driver's seat around?"

I do as instructed and Kait begins bringing the full wall slide in. It takes about 30 seconds to come all the way in and I am amazed at the transformation. When the full wall slide is in, half the living space is gone. However, there is still enough room to walk to the bedroom and access everything in the motorhome, including the bathroom.

Kait heads into the bedroom and brings in the second slide. With both slides in, I notice that the bed has slid partially below the two half closets. "It looks like we lost about 6 inches of the bed because of those closets. Let's see if we can still fit on the bed with the slides in," I say to Kait.

Since we can no longer walk around the bed, Kait crawls across to the left side of the bed and I hop in next to her. "I fit fine," Kait says. "How about you?"

"My feet kind of hit the closet, but I could definitely sleep a night or two like this if we were some place where we couldn't put a slide out. The only problem I see is if you need to get up in the middle of the night, you'd have to crawl over me, but I don't think it's a deal breaker."

We head back into the living room where Ron is waiting for us. "You guys want to take it for a drive?" he asks.

"Sure, let's take it out," I reply.

Ron puts a few things away and makes sure that all of the cabinets and drawers are closed. He holds the keys out. "Who wants to drive first?"

"Let's have Joe drive first," Kait says. "I can drive us back."

On the road, the Bay Star seems to drive a bit better than the other gas motorhomes. It's definitely quieter as I accelerate down the street and towards the freeway. Heading up the on-ramp, I gun the engine a bit to see how quickly we can get to speed. The Bay Star has the same Ford V10 engine as the other gas motorhomes so the acceleration is no different. Ron explains that this model is built on the same 22,000 pound chassis as the Southwind we've been looking at. Since this is a shorter and therefore lighter motorhome, it has about double the carrying capacity of the Southwind. That's why the Bay Star drives more like the Southwind and less like the Flair, on a 16,000 pound chassis.

A few miles down the freeway, Ron has me exit and pull over to hand the reins over to Kait. She gets right back on the freeway and guns it just like I did.

"I hope you guys learn to manage those lead feet, otherwise you're going to have quite the gas bill," Ron says chuckling.

We make it back to the dealership and ask Ron if we can be alone in the motorhome for a while to talk. He obliges and heads back into his office.

"So what'd you think?" I ask Kait.

"I love it. It felt like home when we first walked in and I knew this was the one."

"I feel the same way. My only two issues is it doesn't have that L-shaped couch and the front TV is kind of worthless because there isn't a good place to watch it. Aside from that I think it's perfect for us. What do you think about the price?"

"The price is good, but I think there should still be a little bit of room to negotiate."

"So you want to go in and see what we can work out with Ron?"

"Let's do it!" Kait exclaims.

Inside the sales office, which, incidentally is a converted RV trailer, we sit down and tell Ron that we're interested, but need to discuss the price. The MSRP is $132,000 and the offer on the table is for $105,000.

"We'd like to offer $98,000 for it."

Ron looks at me for a second and says, "We can do $102,000. That's how much we need to make a profit and we can't go any lower than that."

I look over at Kait and she has a blank expression on her face. I can't get any read on her and what she thinks of Ron's offer.

"How is your credit?" Ron asks.

"Great," and I tell him what our scores are.

"Do you have a loan approved?"

"Yes we do," and I tell him the rate we got. I am pretty proud because it was less than anything else I could find.

"Here is what we can do for you. Like I said, $102,000 is the lowest we can go, but I can guarantee you a lower rate with our bank. That will save you a bit more money. What do you guys think?"

I look over at Kait and her face is still completely blank. I don't know if she is upset Ron won't come down to our price or if she's just spacing out. "Babe, what do you think?" I ask.

Kait doesn't respond and just kind of looks over at me. I'm panicking a bit because I can normally read her like a book, but at this moment I have no idea what, if anything, is going through her head. We both love the Bay Star and the offer gets us another few thousand off the price plus a better rate on the loan. It all works out in my head, but Kait seems totally unresponsive and it looks like I am going to need to be the one to make the decision.

"We'll take it!" I say to Ron, extending my hand across the desk.

He shakes my hand and when I look over at Kait, she seems to have come out of her state. I see her reach over and shake Ron's hand, but I have no idea if she's happy about the deal. I made what I thought was the right decision. Ron explains that it will take about a week to get the Bay Star all set up and we can pick it up next weekend. He reaches into a file cabinet and pulls out all of the paperwork for us to sign.

"We'd like to go through the Bay Star top to bottom and write down any issues we find. We're willing to put a deposit down today, but we won't sign the paperwork until we're satisfied that everything on our list has been fixed," I say to Ron.

"That's not a problem, we just ask for a $2,000 deposit that will be returned if you aren't satisfied when you come back to take delivery."

Ron hands me a piece of paper and a pen so we can make our list while Kait goes into the Jeep to grab the checklist we put together. It lists everything we want to check in and around the motorhome.

"Hey what happened back in the office?" I ask Kait as we walk back into the Bay Star.

"What do you mean?" She asks.

"What do I mean? I mean the part where I was negotiating with Ron and you spaced out!"

"Oh that, I was fine with the price and you were negotiating, so I kind of spaced out for a second."

"So you're fine with the deal we made?"

"Of course!"

"Whew, I was worried there for a moment because I didn't know what to think, your face was blank and you weren't giving me any feedback."

"Oh sorry. Good job honey, I'm very happy with the deal we got," Kait says with a huge smile on her face.

The next hour is spent going through every nook and cranny of the motorhome. Since we started shopping, we've seen too many new motorhomes with all sorts of blatant issues. Broken doors, wallpaper peeling off, missing trim pieces and a number of other things. Going through the Newmar is a breath of fresh air. We find a few minor issues, but overall the Bay Star is in great shape. We return to Ron's office with a short list of items to be addressed. Ron looks the list over and assures us they'll all be taken care of when we take delivery next weekend. Ron has me fill out the loan application as Kait writes a check for the $2,000 deposit.

"Holy cow! We just bought a motorhome," Kait says once we're back in the Jeep. The look on her face is a mixture of excitement and terror.

"I can't believe it, but honestly I feel good about this," I tell her. "I know it's the right motorhome for us and is almost exactly what we wanted, plus I think we got a great deal."

"I know, but I am going to be freaking out about this for a while, just like I did when we bought the house."

"Oh, I know you will," I say with a big smile on my face. "Just don't go back online and start looking at other motorhomes, promise?"

"Promise," Kait says.

16. TAKING DELIVERY

Tuesday, June 16th, 2015

Each week feels longer than the previous one. Last week dragged by and somehow this week is going even slower. Saturday can't come soon enough as I anticipate taking delivery of our 2015 Newmar Bay Star 2903. I'm trying to stay sane by researching the devices and gadgets that we'll need to be ready for the road.

The first thing on my list is an electrical management system (EMS), which is a high tech device that protects against more than just power surges. Considering we're paying over $100,000 for our new motorhome, the last thing I want is for it to get fried because of a power surge. I've also read that some campgrounds experience brownouts or low voltage situations. This happens when everyone turns on their A/C in the afternoon and the electrical system at the park buckles under the load if it's antiquated or not well maintained. Low voltage can screw up some of the systems on a motorhome so the EMS will protect from that as well. The EMS is around $300, but I see it as an insurance policy that is well worth the investment.

The second item is the Garmin 760 LMT. This is an RV specific GPS that takes into account the parameters of the RV (height, length, width and weight) when planning a route. It will help us avoid low bridges, restricted roads and even toll roads. The new motorhome is to be 12'8" tall and I don't want to peel the roof off going under a low bridge. Kait is my "GPS" now and sometimes...well, let's just say I end up making a lot of wrong turns when she's navigating.

"What did you buy this time?" Kait asks pointing to an Amazon box as I walk in the door.

"Oh, that should be the sewer hose connection I picked up for us," I say with a big smile. As unexciting as a sewer hose connection is, it's been like Christmas with all the stuff I've ordered and I'm excited to open the box. As I pull the Benchmade knife from my pocket to open the box, Kait walks over and gives me the "look."

"No more buying anything until we get the motorhome. We don't even have it and you're buying all this stuff. Let's wait until we get it home and decide what we need before you buy anything else. Ron said he would provide upgraded hoses, RV toilet paper and sewer connections for us when we pick up the Bay Star this weekend."

"Okay, fine." I knew this was coming because it's not the first time she's had to stop me from buying gear. It seems like every time I get into a new hobby, I end up buying all the equipment I think I'll need before I even start. In that respect, I'm a lot like my father. At least I know where I get it. She does make a great point however. We're going to be limited by the amount of stuff we can bring and there's no reason to buy anything unless it's essential. I guess this is not a good time to tell her about the EMS and GPS that are on their way.

Kait mentions that we will need to adopt a one-in-one-out rule when we're living in the motorhome. If we buy something, we'll have to get rid of something else in its place. That way we don't accumulate too much and end up storing things that never get used. I wish we had implemented that policy in the house. It would make this minimizing process much easier. In the house, it seems like there is always a closet, shelf or drawer to put something in. In the motorhome, we're not only going to be limited on space, but also by weight. After the weight of water, the two of us, the boys and the Jeep, we'll end up with around 2,500 pounds of carrying capacity for all our "things."

Saturday, June 20th, 2015

It's early and we're ready to head over and pick up the Bay Star. I got an email from Ron yesterday letting us know it is ready and we can stop by anytime, but should plan on spending a few hours there. One of the techs is going to perform a full walk-through of the Bay Star, its systems, and answer our questions. I let him know we'll be there when they open so we can have the whole day if we need it.

"Honey, is your phone charged?" Kait asks once we get in the Jeep to head to the dealership.

"It is, did you charge yours?"

"I did. I want to make sure we have a backup in case mine dies while we're filming the walk-through. I read that it's easy to get completely overwhelmed and some people suggested filming it for reference later. I'll have you do the walk-through with the tech since you understand that stuff better and I will film it."

When we arrive at the lot, our Bay Star is parked up front, washed, waxed and ready to go. "Our new home looks great!" Kait exclaims.

"Hey Joe, hey Kait." Ron greets us from the doorway of the sales office. "Why don't we finish all of your paperwork and then I'll have Jack take you on your walk-through."

"Sounds good," I say, "but before we start with the paperwork, I'd like to go through the list of issues we found and make sure those have been addressed."

"No problem, I'll be in here when you're ready. The Bay Star is unlocked so go right in."

Kait has the list and is reading off each item. "Broken trim piece on corner of bathroom wall,"

"Looks like they replaced that, check," I respond.

"Back burner didn't light."

I turn the knob for the rear burner and it fires to life. "Looks good."

We spend the next 15 minutes going through the list and find that the last item wasn't fixed. Kait does not look happy about it.

"So what do you want to do? Walk away from the deal and take our deposit back?" I ask.

"No, let's go talk to Ron and see what he has to say."

"Hey Ron, everything looks good except the rear bay door still isn't closing properly," I tell him.

"Hey Jack!" Ron shouts and a shorter gentleman runs into the office.

"What's up Ron?"

"The list that the Russos gave us to check, still has one open item. They said the bay door still isn't closing properly. Did you look at that?"

"No, I meant to ask them when they pulled up. I wasn't sure which door it was so I wanted to confirm before I messed with any of them."

I head outside and show Jack the door in question. He says he can fix it with a simple adjustment of the latch and will have it done before we're finished with the paperwork.

"That works for me," Kait says when she sees me look over for approval.

For the price of this motorhome, we could have bought a house or a piece of land and it dawns on me that the paperwork we have to sign is a fraction of what we had to sign when we purchased our house. Once everything is official, we head out to meet Jack for the walk-through. The point of the walk-through is to go through the entire motorhome and get familiar with all of the systems, learn how things work and, hopefully, get some pointers for minor trouble shooting.

As promised, Jack has the bay door working properly and we follow him into the bedroom to begin our education. Kait is ready to record the entire experience and I'm ready to be a sponge. We start in the bedroom and Jack is showing us where all of the light switches are and then opens a cabinet to walk us through how the Blu-Ray player and TV work.

"Can we test the Blu-Ray player to make sure it works? I brought a DVD to try," Kait asks.

Laughing, Jack says, "That's the first time anyone has ever brought a DVD to try on a walk-through. Hand it over and we can make sure it works."

Kait pulls it out of her purse, handing it to Jack. "I love *Animal House*. Maybe we should just hang out in here and watch the movie," he jokes.

We all have a good laugh and then get back to the walk-through. There is so much to learn; I'm happy we are filming it. I have a feeling that my future self will be thanking Kait for recording everything. We go through basics like where all of the light switches are (some are not so obvious) and even how to work the toilet. Not something I ever thought I would need someone to explain, but an RV toilet is very different from the one in our house. "We're planning on removing the toilet and putting in a composting toilet," Kait tells Jack.

"I've heard about those but I've never seen one." Jack looks back toward the bedroom and says, "It's my favorite part of the movie." He gets up and quickly makes his way back to the bedroom.

John Belushi's character, Bluto, is sitting at a table with trays full of food in front of him when he says, "See if you can guess what I am now? A zit! Get it?"

We all laugh at the classic scene and then Jack starts walking us through critical systems such as how to operate the hydraulic jacks and locking/unlocking the slides. Jack gives us a serious warning to make sure the slide is unlocked before putting it out, repeating it several times, suggesting we put a sticky note next to the button as a reminder. The concern is that the slide is powerful enough to damage the walls of the motorhome if we leave the slide locked, doing tens of thousands of dollars worth of damage, something he's seen before. Outside, he walks us through how to dump the gray and black holding tanks and provides us with an upgraded sewer hose kit. Turns out Kait was right and we may not need some of the things I had on my list to buy.

About two hours later, I think I can at least get this thing home in one piece. Kait decides to follow me in the Jeep and we talk through which route to take so we can avoid tight streets and traffic. As I sit down in the driver's seat, my heart is racing. It's one thing to test-drive a motorhome, but it's quite another to actually drive one we bought. The next year of our lives depends on having this motorhome and if I screw up and crash it before we even get home, that dream could be delayed for quite a while.

I pull out of the lot and as I begin to make the turn, I hear a crashing noise behind me, and turn to see that most of the kitchen drawers have flown open. They have catches that lock the drawers in place, but I forgot to make sure they were all pushed in and locked. I also forgot to put away the remotes and those are now spread out across the floor. Putting the hazard lights on I pull over, jumping out of my seat to shut all of the drawers when I hear Kait open the door.

"Everything all right in here?"

"Yeah, it's fine. I forgot to check all of the drawers and make sure everything was put away."

Kait smiles and heads back to the Jeep. I do a quick check of the rest of the motorhome finding the shower door also needs to be latched. On my way back to the front, I grab the TV and stereo remotes, but I can't find the DVD remote. Looks like it may have slid under the slide and I make a mental note to look for it when we get home.

The rest of the drive is uneventful. The longer I drive, the more comfortable I become. The side view cameras are coming in handy to make sure I stay in the lane and see what is next to me. Driving something that's nine feet wide takes some getting used to. It's also hard to judge the height of the motorhome and I am concerned about hitting a low hanging branch. It's a good thing I have that RV GPS on order. Jack told us to be careful because there are delicate systems on the roof including the A/C unit that could get damaged from a branch. The roof is skinned with a special kind of rubber so we also have to be careful not to tear it. It's a lot to be aware of while trying to keep this thing between the dotted lines. I'm relieved when I finally pull up in front of the house.

We live in a cul-de-sac and our house is at the very end of the street. There should be enough room for me to do a three-point turn and back into our 45-foot long driveway. It's nice that we can fit the motorhome and Jeep in the driveway, but Kait's Honda will have to live on the street until we sell it.

Kait parks a few houses down and walks over to be my spotter. The driveway is narrow with a tree and small picket fence on one side. She gets in position and I start to make my turn. This is the first time I've backed up a motorhome and it's pretty easy using a combination of the rear camera and mirrors. The problem I have is that I can't get a good visual of the tree branches to know if they will clear the roof and I'm happy to have an extra set of eyes. Not only can I see Kait in the passenger side mirror but I can hear her as well. Our rear camera has a microphone so I can hear her giving me commands as she starts waving me back, watching the tree to make sure I won't hit it. I do a quick check of the driver's side mirror and slam on the brakes. Kait was so focused on the tree that she didn't see I was about to hit the curb. I pull forward, align the driver's side of the motorhome with the edge of the driveway and start making my way back again, getting into the driveway without any other problems.

"Do you want to get us level?" Kait asks.

"Sure, let's see if I remember how to do this. Engine on, parking brake set and press the Auto Level button."

I hear the hydraulic whine of the jacks slowly lowering. Once the first pair touch the ground, the Bay Star does a dance as it raises and levels itself. I've read that it's best to level the motorhome manually, but until I have a better handle on the system, I'll stick with the self-leveling feature. The control panel beeps at me once it's level.

"Let's put the slides out," I say. "Did you check to see if we will clear the bushes?"

"It looks like you should be okay. Let me go outside, and keep an eye on them. Don't forget to make sure that the slides are unlocked."

Kait walks around to the driver's side while I check the slide locks, confirm they're unlocked, then push the slide out button. Nothing happens. I push it again. Nothing. "Damn it, what am I forgetting?" I check to make sure that the motorhome is in park, the engine is off with the key out of the ignition, and double check that the arms are unlocked. Everything seems to be in order so I push the button again. Nothing.

"What's going on?" Kait asks as she walks back inside.

"The slide isn't working. I don't know why. It worked fine at the dealership when we put them out and brought them back in. Can you think of anything I am missing?"

"You checked to make sure the motorhome was in park and we have enough battery to put the slides out?"

"Ah I forgot the battery, let me check." The battery monitor shows it's fully charged. "I guess that's not it." I push the button for the slide again and still nothing.

"Why don't you call Jack? He said if we ever have any questions to give him a call," Kait reminds me.

I'm your typical guy. I don't like to ask for directions or help. I want to figure everything out on my own, but Kait has a point. My pride isn't worth breaking something so I dial the cell number Jack wrote on his card.

"Hey Jack, this is Joe Russo. Sorry to bother you, but we're having a problem with the big slide and I can't get it out."

"Okay, your jacks are down and the motorhome is in park, correct?"

"Yes. I also checked to make sure none of the locking arms were engaged, but nothing happens when I push the slide out button."

"Did you hold the button down? The button has to be held down for a few seconds before the slide will start to go out, it's a safety feature."

"Uh, no I didn't. Let me try that." I reach out and hold down the button. A few long seconds go by and then the slide starts going out. "Yep, that worked," I chuckle. "Thanks Jack and sorry to bother you."

"No problem, Joe. There is a lot of stuff to learn so feel free to call anytime if you have questions."

A few minutes later Kait and I have the motorhome all set up in the driveway. "Should we bring the boys in?" I ask.

"Sure, but we should put some blankets down for Leo since he's afraid of slippery floors and maybe put Duke's harness on to help him in. His hind legs have been bothering him lately and I don't want him to fall the first time he comes in here."

"Good idea, I'll get the boys ready. I'm nervous that they won't want to come inside."

When I bring the boys outside, they are reluctant to climb the stairs into the motorhome. "I have an idea," Kait says walking outside. "Give me the boys and you go inside and call them."

Once I'm at the top of the stairs, Duke and Leo have no problem following me in and proceed to sniff every square inch of the place before they settled down.

It's another hot day, so I get the generator started and turn the A/C on. The motorhome uses a 30 amp, 120V electrical connection which aren't standard in homes. I have an adapter that will allow me to plug into a standard wall outlet. Those are only 15amps, not enough to run the A/C, so the generator needs to be running. Kait goes into the house and returns with two cold beers. "Cheers and congratulations!"

"Thanks babe, you read my mind. I needed this," I say taking a long sip off the Modelo she brought me. "So when do you want to move in?"

"I want to get the composting toilet installed before we move in."

17. THE BUCKET THRONE

Sunday, June 28th, 2015

For months we've been researching composting toilets. Kait has been reading horror stories about dumping the RV tanks with many going into gruesome detail. Most people don't think about that aspect of RVing, but everything that goes down a drain or the toilet ends up in the gray or black tank. Both need to be emptied frequently depending on the size of the tanks and how quickly they are filled.

Of course, Kait has been sharing stories of how people mis-connect the sewer pipe and end up with the "contents" from the black tank all over the place and themselves. It reminds me of the scene from the Robin Williams movie *RV* where he ends up covering himself in the black tank contents. I get queasy just thinking about it.

This is why composting toilets got our attention. They work by diverting the solid and liquid waste into separate compartments within the toilet, eliminating the need for a black tank. The liquid waste goes into a container that can be dumped into a public toilet. The solid waste goes into a chamber with some type of medium, typically coconut husk, which absorbs the moisture from the waste, rendering it virtually odor free. When the chamber fills up a few weeks later we can dump the contents into a trash bag and deposit that in the dumpster.

Horror stories aside, there are other benefits of a composting toilet. We can go much longer between dumping the tanks because we will only be filling the gray tank. Some

RVers even repurpose the black tank to act as a secondary gray tank which would allow us to stay off-grid that much longer.

"Do you want me to order the composting toilet?"

"How much is it?" Kait asks.

"The one we are looking at is about $1,000."

"Are you sure you can install it?"

"It looks simple enough, but I need to make sure I can route the vent properly."

"Why do we need a vent?"

"Well the toiler has a small electric fan that vents any odors outside and helps dry the solid waste."

"Do we have to plug the toilet in then?"

"Not exactly. I'll have to run wires from the toilet to a spot in the motorhome with 12 volt power."

"Let's make sure you can install it before we order anything."

It's the end of June and blistering hot out. With the A/C on, the motorhome is nice and cool so I'm tempted to just sit in here and relax, but I need to get this done today so I can order the toilet and install it next weekend. We're going to have the house on the market soon and I would like to have us moved in before that happens.

The bathroom is small with enough room to stand in front of the sink or sit on the toilet, but not both. The sink is in the middle of the room with a decent amount of counter space. Surprisingly, there is a good amount of storage with a medicine cabinet above the sink, a cabinet along the wall to the right of the sink and a deep cabinet under the sink along with a pull out drawer that doubles as a step stool. Standing in the bathroom looking around, I say to myself, "trying to live in this small space is going to be difficult." Not sure if I am having regrets or just need some time to adjust to the space, but I remember I have a job to do.

The composting toilet is quite a bit longer and wider with its two tanks. I need to measure and make sure it will fit in place of our current toilet without blocking access to anything. My tape measure confirms that it will be tight, but I should be able to squeeze it in without any problems. Getting down on my knees, I inspect the area below the sink looking for a way to route the vent and wires into the bays below. The hot and cold water lines are routed up through the floor in the back of the cabinet and it looks like I should be able to drill a hole that will get me into the bays while keeping everything hidden. It doesn't look like it should be too difficult to get the toilet installed so I shut down the A/C and generator to head back into the house. As I am locking the door, I look over at the bays and a little voice in the back of my head tells me I should check to see how they routed the water lines coming up through the bathroom floor.

The bathroom is located on the passenger side and I walk about halfway down the length of the motorhome and open the bay I think is under the bathroom. I don't see any of the water lines I expected to see. The bay to the left of this one houses the generator, but I open it anyway. As I expected, this bay is simply a big box with the generator and nothing else. I open the bay further to the right, no water lines. I head back into the motorhome and measure how far the water lines are from the front of the motorhome. Heading back outside, I spool the tape measure out from the front of the motorhome and walk it back, stopping next to the rear wheels, to the right of the generator bay. That can't be right. After some more prodding in the bays, I find the water lines routed in a small gap between the floor and the top of the wheel well. There's no way I can access that area. Covered in sweat and in dire need of ice water and a shower, I head back into the house.

"How did it go?" Kait asks.

"The toilet would be a tight fit, but that doesn't matter because I can't find a way to route the vent and wiring. The only way to make it work would be to drill a hole through the side or roof of the motorhome and I don't think we want to do either."

"No way, but that's all right. While you were outside I was researching bucket toilets."

"Bucket toilets? Please don't tell me you want us to poop in a bucket."

Kait is so excited at this point she's bouncing on the couch. "Listen, I found this book by Joseph Jenkins called *The Humanure Handbook*. It talks about all the environmental issues of using standard toilets and about how you can make a bucket toilet to use instead. Here, read this quote."

Kait hands over her computer and I read the quote out loud, "The world is divided into two categories of people: those who shit in drinking water and those who don't."

I hand the computer back to Kait and she gives me a very serious look, "I don't want to shit into our water supply anymore."

"Babe, you're crazy and there's no way I am going to have a bucket for a toilet in our brand new hundred thousand dollar motorhome."

"Will you at least read about it and maybe we can give it a try?"

"Sure, but after I take a shower."

Later that night I go online and start reading about these bucket toilets. They are pretty popular with people who are out in the sticks and don't have access to traditional plumbing or are limited on their water supply, mostly off-grid cabins. People say they work great, don't smell and are just a simplified version of the $1,000 composting toilets we're looking to buy. The biggest difference is that the bucket toilet doesn't have a way to divert the liquids into a separate container. It also doesn't use any kind of vents or fans. Take a standard five-gallon bucket, put a trash bag inside, fill it with some type of medium and go to town. A lot of people enclose them in a box with a toilet seat and lid. Call me crazy, but this sounds like it might work. Heading to bed, I find Kait awake and looking at something on her phone. "Let me guess, you're researching bucket toilets."

"There are a lot of people who use them and say they don't smell and work well. I think this could work for us."

"I've been reading up on them too."

"And?"

"And I think it might work, but I'm still hesitant about the idea."

"Can we at least try it? Do you think you can make something for us to keep the bucket in and sit on when we go to the bathroom?"

Kait is playing to my weak side. I'll take any excuse to go to the home improvement store for supplies to build something, even if that thing is a bucket toilet.

"Okay, but I'll need do some more research this week. Next weekend we can pick up the supplies and I'll put something together."

Kait is so excited that I doubt she'll be getting to bed any time soon. I have my doubts. The idea of saving nearly a grand by making our own toilet is appealing, but will it actually work for us?

Saturday, July 4th, 2015

I'm greeted by hundreds of BBQs on sale outside the home improvement store. I walk through the door and make my way to the lumber section, grabbing a large sheet of 1/2-inch plywood and a long piece of 1"x1" trim. Walking down a few more aisles, I grab a bag of angle brackets, some hinges, a nice toilet seat, a package of felt furniture pads and, of course, a five-gallon bucket. I also pick up a gripper plug and a few other things in the plumbing department. As I am waiting in line at the register, I notice the guy next to me eyeing my cart. "Got some home improvement projects to get done this weekend?" He asks.

"I don't know if it would be considered an improvement, but I've certainly got my work cut out for me." If only the guy knew what my plans were for everything I'm buying.

Back at the house, I clear some space in the garage and get to work. The plan is to make something simple yet functional with easy access to change out the trash bag in the bucket. After about an hour, the four sides of the toilet are squared up and screwed together.

I cut a few lengths of the 1"x1" trim and screw those into the bottom of the toilet as legs. Next, I take another piece of plywood and set it inside the box to use as a base for the bucket with a few pieces of scrap wood to hold the bucket in place. With the bucket centered, I trace the lip of the bucket on the last piece of plywood and use my jigsaw to cut the hole out, mount it to the box with the hinges and then install the toilet seat over the hole. Sitting on the toilet, I find it's surprisingly comfortable and solid as a rock. As I am sitting on my handmade throne, I look over and see paint left over from another project and put a few coats on the new "toilet." I must say, it looks pretty good for a few hours worth of work.

Kait walks out with a glass of ice water just as I finish. "Wow you're done, and you painted it red."

"Yep I decided it needed a bit of polish."

"I love it! When can you put it in the motorhome?"

"I still need to remove the toilet, but once that's done I can put this in there and the paint should be dry by then."

"Do you realize this bucket toilet is red, white and blue and it just so happens to be Independence Day weekend?"

"I didn't even think about that. I present our independence bucket toilet!"

In the bathroom, I remove two bolts at the base of the toilet; pull the water line off, lift the entire toilet right out and carry it outside. Back in the bathroom, I install the 3-inch gripper plug to block off the drain to the black tank and plug the water line. Don't want the bathroom to flood every time we turn on the water pump. With that done, the new toilet is ready to come in.

"Smile honey!" Kait is standing next to the motorhome with the camera as I am trying to maneuver the bucket toilet through the door.

"Babe, I'm hot, sweaty and carrying a toilet made out of plywood. Now might not be the time to take pictures."

"But I want to write about this and I need a picture of you taking the new toilet into the motorhome."

I hold the bucket toilet up for Kait as she snaps off a few pictures and carefully walk up the steps into the motorhome with our new throne.

Aside from the felt pads I put on the bottom of the legs to protect the bathroom tiles, there is no installation. Just drop it where the old one was. According to the research Kait has done, pine shavings should work well in our new toilet as a medium to absorb moisture. It just so happens we have half a bag left in the garage from when we raised chickens. I grab that along with a trash bag to line the bucket. I fill the bag about a quarter of the way with shavings to start. The only thing left now is to break in the toilet and I've had a lot of water. It's a bit strange peeing into a bucket full of pine shavings, but I better get used to it.

"Now that we have the bucket toilet in, I'd like to move into the motorhome," Kait says, handing me another glass of ice water.

"Sure, but let's do it tomorrow. We need to get ready for the fireworks tonight."

18. MOVIN' IN

On July 4th, our neighborhood turns into a war zone. Fireworks are outlawed in the greater Los Angeles area due to the danger of wildfires, but no one cares around here. We can hear small poppers to professional level mortars going off all day. It doesn't matter that the sun is still out; our neighbors love their fireworks. There is even one neighbor who has a grenade launcher that he uses to shoot flares into the sky.

Duke was afraid of everything when we brought him home. It was painful watching him walk down a residential street because he would cower every time a car drove by. Now, he can prance down a major street with the trash truck right next to him without blinking, but fireworks still scare him to death. We've learned to stay in, put on a loud movie and close all the windows and blinds. He's usually pretty good with our routine until we go to sleep. We try to stay up as late as possible but at 1 a.m. we're ready for bed. The fireworks seem to have calmed down a bit, and after the day I had installing the new toilet, I'm looking forward to passing out on our plush latex mattress. The neighbors, on the other hand, have other plans and another volley of fireworks go off. "Damn it." I say under my breath as Duke jumps off his bed and begins pacing through the house.

"It's going to be a rough night for everyone in this household," I say to Kait. "Why don't you crawl into bed and keep Leo company. I'll stay in the living room with Duke."

"Thanks honey. Don't stay up too much longer."

I put the TV back on and Duke comes over and puts his head on my lap and then his left paw. I know where this is going so I pat my chest. Duke stands up, sliding the rest of his body onto my lap, leaving his hind legs on the ground and curls himself up as best he can. With Duke comfortable, I close my eyes and wake up about an hour later to find that Duke has gotten the rest of himself on the couch and is passed out next to me. "Come on bud, time to head to bed. It's been a long night for both of us."

Duke slides off my lap and leads the way to the bedroom. Kait and Leo are both sound asleep as I slide into bed next to Kait. I'm going to miss this bed. The one in the Bay Star isn't very comfortable and it's only a queen. We've had this king bed for about two years and I like having the extra room. Kait does some serious karate moves in her sleep and, when we had our queen bed, I was too often on the receiving end. The extra space in the king gives me a buffer, but in a queen, I'm not sure I'll have room to escape her elbow of death.

That morning we're both able to sleep in a bit. Duke is worn out from last night and decided to let me sleep in until 10 a.m. before nudging me awake. "Morning bud. Feeling better today?" Duke responds with a wagging tail and a cold nose under the covers. "Okay, okay I'm getting up."

"Is it time to get up already?" Kait asks as she stretches and pulls the comforter up over her head.

"Yep, we've got to move into the motorhome today. Last night of sleeping in the house."

"Oh, I almost forgot. I'm up! Let's get this party started boys."

It's amazing how much energy Kait has in the morning. My gears don't start turning until I've had that first cup of coffee and even then I am sluggish. It's strange to get up, walk into the living room and see this giant motorhome parked in the driveway. Kind of like that first morning seeing yourself in the mirror after a new haircut, at least from what I remember. It's been a long time since I even had hair, let alone a haircut.

The dining area and living room are a mess and have been since the garage sale. We've turned the space into a staging area to help us visualize the amount of stuff we want to bring with us. Most of what we have out are clothes, but we've also put together the kitchen and bathroom items we want to bring. Kait's approach has been to take the absolute least possible while mine has been to try and bring as much as possible. My thinking is that we have no idea what living out of a motorhome is going to be like. Why not bring as much as possible and figure out what we can get rid of later than look back and wish we had kept certain things. Kait figures we'll be fine with two place settings of cutlery, one pot, one pan and a chef's knife.

Once my coffee is ready, I take my first cup and make my way through the jungle of stuff to the couch and clear off a spot to sit. There's nothing like that first sip of coffee in the morning and I just sit there for a few minutes savoring it. Feeling more human, I set the cup down on a mahjong set because there isn't any open space on the coffee table. As I sit there, I can't stop thinking about the bed situation. We bought our current mattress because of my back pain and it has helped quite a bit. I've been trying to figure out how to keep it and this morning the coffee seems to be fueling my imagination.

"Babe!" I shout. Kait is still in the bedroom and walks out with another load of clothes.

"What? Why are you shouting?"

"I have a great idea. How would you like to get rid of the mattress in the motorhome and keep the one we have?"

"Uh, I would love to, but that's a king and we only have room for a queen."

"A trivial point my dear. I think I've figured out a way for us to keep the mattress."

"Okay, you work on that. I'm going to start moving stuff into the motorhome. I'm better at organizing that stuff anyway and there are certain places I want to put things."

"Just remember to leave some space for all of my coffee gear."

"How could I forget?"

I grab my coffee and head into the motorhome while Kait is still trying to figure out what she wants to move in first. The "upgraded" queen mattress that came with the motorhome is thin and way too firm. It's still wrapped in plastic so I figure we can try and sell it on Craigslist. I grab my tape measure and verify that the mattress is indeed a residential queen. The problem with many RV beds is that they can be smaller than their residential counterparts making it a pain to replace them. Underneath the mattress, is a flat platform that should work well for what I have planned. Along each side of the bed there are small nightstands that are fixed to the wall with a permanently mounted headboard. I make a few notes and head back into the house. The first thing I grab is a large chef's knife that Kait has put in the "ditch" pile and a black Sharpie from another pile.

In the bedroom, I strip the sheets and mattress protector off the bed. My plan would never have worked if we got the innerspring mattress, but I think this should work with the latex mattress. It cost us over $2,000 so I am a bit reluctant, but it's going in the dumpster otherwise. I mark the bed with the Sharpie according to the measurements I took. After measuring twice, I plunge the knife into the mattress and start sawing.

"Hey babe, come in here and check this out!" I shout ten minutes later.

"Oh interesting. You cut the mattress down to a queen?"

"Kind of, I call this a queen plus. What I did was cut the head of the mattress so it would fit in between the nightstands and then flared it out so it's about six inches wider than a normal queen. It might be a bit hard to find sheets, but I thought this would work better than the mattress in there now."

"Honey, that's great! Do you want me to help you move out the mattress that's in there and then we can move this one in?"

"Sure, I'm curious to see how well it fits."

We get the RV mattress out in no time, but getting the "queen plus" in is a whole other story. We have a difficult time maneuvering it up the stairs and into the bedroom. I forgot how heavy this thing is, but once it's in place, I'm impressed. The bed fits like a glove, but it's about twice as thick as the mattress we pulled out. I'm concerned the mattress might not fit underneath the closets when the slides are in. I guess I can always try and stuff it under the closet as the slide is coming in or break out the knife and do some more trimming. Either way, our mattress is now in and I feel much better about sleeping in the motorhome.

I spend the rest of the day helping Kait carry things in while she finds a place for them. There's a common saying in the RVing community, "there's a place for everything, and everything has its place." We each have our own cabinets and drawers for clothes and to maximize space, Kait refolded all of my shirts and somehow managed to fit twice as many in the drawers than I could. All of that space I thought we had is quickly being used up. Kait was right, I need to cut way back on how much stuff I bring.

"Why don't you tell me where you want things and I'll put them away for you," Kait says.

"I won't argue with that," I say looking down at the trash bag Kait has next to her. "What's in there?"

"Oh, those are the socks I was going to throw away. I'm going to use them to put fragile items in so they don't rattle or break as we drive down the road. Do you have any I can use?"

"That's brilliant. I have a bunch of socks I was going to get rid of so I'll bring them in for you."

I'm always amazed at the things that woman comes up with. She has a few other tricks up her sleeves for repurposing items we were going to discard like lining the pantry drawers with old cloth placemats so the items don't scratch the wood. The next few hours are spent moving everything we think we'll need inside. I told Kait I wanted to hold off on trying to load up the bays until we have a better idea of what's going in them. There are items that we won't need access to right away like all of our winter clothes, and they've been packed into smaller suitcases and backpacks to be stored in the bays.

While Kait is working on sorting out the bathroom, I decide to get dinner started. We haven't moved any of our food into the motorhome, so I head back inside and grab a package of hot Italian sausages and a couple cans of diced tomatoes. Kait's already moved the spices, and finding them turns out to be a challenge.

"Kait, I need some help in here. I don't know where you put anything."

"What are you looking for?"

"The large pot and the spices."

"The pot is in the drawer under the fridge and the spices are in that big drawer under the stove."

Everything is exactly where she says it is, but it's going to take some time getting accustomed to the new layout. I'll need to adjust quickly because starting today; we'll be living strictly out of the motorhome. This way we can start painting and getting the house ready to sell. The lawn is coming in nicely and John is eager to get the property listed as soon as we are ready.

I drop the sausages into the pan, cover them with water and turn the stove on high. Once the water is boiling and the sausages are pretty much cooked, I turn the stove down and let the water cook down a bit. What's left is a sausage broth. I throw in the two cans of diced tomatoes, a chopped onion, chopped peppers, beans, garlic, spices and a splash of red wine. It's a simple comfort dish I can make without any help from Kait. I thought it would be the perfect first meal in the motorhome together.

"Dinner is ready," I tell Kait.

"Perfect timing, I just finished putting things away in the bathroom."

"I forgot to tell you, but I already christened the new toilet."

"I'm not surprised" Kait says and lets out a little laugh as she looks over my shoulder. I turn around and see Duke perched up on the windowsill watching us.

"Now that we have everything put away, we should bring the boys back in and let them get acclimated," Kait says. "Let's also feed them dinner in here once we're finished eating."

By the time the boys get settled and we're ready to stop working, it's almost 10 p.m. Tomorrow is a workday and we are wiped out from this weekend. "I don't know about you," I tell Kait, "but I am ready to crawl into bed and pass out."

"Me too, but we still need sheets on the bed."

"I forgot all about that. What are we going to do for sheets?"

"I have an idea," Kait says and heads back into the house. A few minutes later she comes back with two of the sheets we used on the king bed and the comforter.

"No fitted sheet?" I ask.

"The king sized fitted sheet is going to be too big and a queen will be too small. I think we can use a regular sheet and tuck it under the mattress."

We get the bed made and the boys have found their spots. Leo is beside me and Duke is at the foot of the bed. Kait opens a few windows, pulls the blackout shades down and I am asleep as soon as my head hits the pillow.

19. WHAT'S THAT SMELL?

Monday, July 6th, 2015

My alarm goes off at 6:30 a.m. and I am reluctant to crawl out of bed. Duke is nudging me to go out so I throw on some clothes, grab his leash and head out of the motorhome for the backyard. Leo is still passed out in a small nook next to Kait's side of the bed. I'm still not sure how he got himself into the tight space, but he seems comfortable. After Duke is done with his morning routine, we head back in the motorhome to find Kait crawling out of bed.

"So, did you use the bucket toilet?" Kait asks.

"No, I went in the house. Did you?"

"I did. It was actually pretty comfortable. You should use it so we can make sure it works."

We agree that, going forward, we'll put the bucket toilet through its paces and avoid using the toilet in the house. After my morning coffee, I'm ready for something I never thought I would do. Poop into a bucket. I'm slightly horrified, but the experience goes over better than I imagined. The toilet is certainly comfortable; glad I sprung for the better toilet seat. Kait has a small box full of pine shavings on the bathroom sink and I scatter them generously over the new content in the bucket. The shavings are supposed to help absorb moisture and prevent odor.

Pulling up to the house that evening after work, I see our neighbor outside.

"Hey Joe!" Juan says. "That's quite the motorhome you've got there."

"Yeah, hard to miss isn't it? We moved in a few days ago and hope to get the house on the market soon. If you guys are free this evening, come on over and we can have a few drinks."

"Sounds great, we'll be over after dinner."

Juan and his family come by at 8pm with a nice bottle of wine as a house warming present. Kait is desperate to get rid of our alcohol so we decide to open the new bottle; at least we're not adding anything to our "stash." As we tell them about our plans, Juan and his wife are still skeptical about what we're doing.

"So you're seriously going to live in here for the next year?" Juan asks.

"That's the plan," Kait responds.

Looking around, Maria says, "I don't know if I could even fit all of my shoes in here, but I'm jealous of this adventure you'll be going on."

"We're excited about it," I tell Maria. "We know it's going to be an adjustment but I'm starting to get used to the space."

"What about all of your clothes?" Maria asks Kait.

"I got rid of most of my clothes and only kept the stuff I wear on a regular basis. The best part, it's a lot easier picking an outfit in the morning."

"Girl, I admire you for that, but there's no way I could do it!"

"I kind of wish she would," Juan whispers to me. "I barely have any room in the closet as it is and most of the stuff she only wears once."

We spend the next couple of hours talking about our plans for the trip and the journey we've gone through to get to this point. It's been over a year since we first came up with this plan and, although we're getting close to the finish line, it feels like we still have a long way to go.

"I'm very happy no one asked to use the bathroom," I tell Kait once everyone has left.

"That would have been an interesting conversation. I wonder what they would have said if we told them to use our bucket?"

"Who knows, just make sure you have a camera rolling if anyone does ask to use it!"

Over the next few days, the bucket toilet seems to be working well until I walk into the motorhome after work on Wednesday. My nose immediately picks up on an odd smell and I have no idea where it's coming from. Walking further into the motorhome I notice the smell is coming from the bathroom. I lift up the lid to the bucket and almost gag. The odor is too much to bear. I immediately pull my shirt over my nose, turn the overhead fan on and head outside to find a second trash bag and a t-shirt. I tie the shirt around my face and, making sure to gently pull out the trash bag in the bucket, I carefully slide it into the second bag. The last thing I need is to have this bag rip open.

Kait pulls up as I am taking the bag to the trash, giving me a strange look. "Why do you have a shirt wrapped around your face?" I don't respond because I am trying to hold my breath as I rush past her to the garbage cans.

"What happened?" She asks.

"I got back from work and the smell coming from the bucket was horrible. I don't think this is going to work."

"Why do you give up so quickly? Let's do some research and see if we can figure out what went wrong. It's not supposed to smell."

That night I make dinner while Kait researches where things went south.

"I think I figured it out," Kait says as she looks up from her computer. "We didn't use enough pine shavings. I think we need to put more in there to start with, and more on top after we go to the bathroom."

"How much more? Won't we fill the toilet a lot faster?"

"Yes, but the problem we are having is the pine shavings aren't soaking up all the fluid and that's why we are getting the smell."

We get the toilet set back up and I add two trash bags to the bucket. The less risk of leaks, the better. Kait fills the bucket with about twice as many pine shavings. It looks like the bucket is almost full but she assures me that they'll sink after a while. A couple days go by and it seems like the new system is working, until I wake up Friday morning and go into the bathroom. The smell isn't as bad as it was on Wednesday, but things are brewing.

"Babe, I have to empty the toilet again, it's starting to smell."

"I wonder why, we used a lot of pine shavings this time."

I take the bag outside and when I get back into the motorhome, Kait is back on her laptop trying to find a solution to our problem.

"Find anything?" I ask.

"Yes, the problem is that we don't have a separate container for the liquids. The mixture of the liquids and solids is what creates the smell. The pine shavings can't soak up enough of the liquid to keep the bucket from smelling. We need untreated sawdust, which should do a much better job."

"Okay, but I've never seen sawdust for sale. We'll have to find a wood shop or lumber yard that might have some."

Kait spends the next thirty minutes calling various places until she gets someone at the local home improvement store. "The person working in lumber told me he'd put a bag of saw dust aside for us, but technically they aren't allowed to give it out to customers. I'm going to head over there now and pick it up."

When she gets home, Kait has a large bag full of sawdust and she pours about a quarter of it into the bucket. The fine saw dust certainly looks more absorbent than the pine shavings. When we're ready to change out the bag in the bucket a few days later, there is very little odor.

"The sawdust seemed to work, but we don't have much left," I tell Kait.

"Yeah, I'm going to have to source some more."

"We're going to need a lot of sawdust. Where are we going to get it once we're on the road?"

"I figure we can find a wood shop or lumber yard and fill up."

"I hate to break your bubble, but we had a tough time finding sawdust in Los Angeles. We can't carry that much with us so what happens when we're in the middle of nowhere and can't find any? Also, if there isn't a place to dump the trash bags, we'll need to load the full trash bags into the Jeep and drive them someplace. I don't even want to imagine what the Jeep would smell like if they leaked. Sorry babe, but I don't think this will work."

Kait looks forlorn at this point. "You're right, I was so inspired by that book that I wanted to try it. Plus I don't want to have to deal with dumping the black tank, everything I've read says it's horrible."

"I don't think it's going to be that bad, plus it can't be any worse than what I had to deal with using the bucket system."

Kait laughs and says, "I guess that means we need to put the other toilet back in."

"I guess it does, but let me have my coffee first and then I'll get it taken care of."

A week later, Kait walks out of the bathroom, looks at me and says, "It's so nice to flush a toilet. I'm sorry the bucket toilet didn't work out. At least it was an interesting experiment."

"Ha! No one can say we didn't try. Now all we have to do is figure out how to dump our tanks."

20. THIRTY DOLLAR DUMP

Tuesday, July 14th, 2015

After living out of the motorhome for over a week, I feel like I am starting to get used to the space. I've tested the shower a few times, but occasionally I still sneak into the house to take a long, hot shower. We've been conservative with our water usage to prevent the waste tanks from filling up too quickly. My RV shower experience is what I would imagine it's like to take a "navy shower." Turn water on, get wet, turn water off, lather, rinse quickly and get out. Gone are the days of just enjoying the hot water running off my back. Even if I wanted to do that, I wouldn't be able to enjoy it for long because our motorhome's water heater only holds six gallons. This morning I stayed a little longer in the shower than I should have and got a nice cold shock when the hot water ran out.

"Joe, there is another smell in here. Do you have any idea where it's coming from?" Kait asks as I come out of the bathroom with a towel wrapped around myself.

"Where is the smell?"

"By the kitchen sink. I don't see anything there that would cause the smell though. Can you come over and check it out?"

"Sure, give me a minute to get dressed."

Heading to the kitchen, I immediately notice the smell as well. "The smell is only in this area. Did you check the trash?"

"Yes. There's nothing in there that would go bad or cause an odor."

"Huh, that's odd. Time to put my nose to work." Kait refers to me as her "Remy" when she needs my nose to do detective work. I'm not sure how I feel about being referred to as a rat from the animated film *Ratatouille*, but she gets a kick out of it every time.

I start sniffing around the kitchen area and stick my head in the sink taking a big breath, which in hindsight was a bad idea. "Well, the smell is definitely coming from the sink. It's draining fine so there isn't anything stuck in there. I'm not sure what would be causing the smell. Did you check the tanks?"

"No, let me check." Kait reaches over and clicks the button for our tank monitor.

"Black tank is at two-thirds and the gray tank is full," she reports.

"My guess is that since we've been filling the gray tank for the last few weeks, and with the 90 degree weather, the water is starting to get a bit rancid. We need to dump the tanks tonight before it gets any worse."

"Let me find a place to dump locally and we can go when you get home from work tonight."

Kait's been working at home a lot more so she has time to work on the motorhome and handle things like this. I've been so swamped at work that I've been taking my lunch to meetings just so I have time to eat. When I get home that night, Kait and the boys are relaxing in the backyard. "What are you guys doing back here?" I say as the boys swarm me for attention. "Have you boys been enjoying the sun?" I say to both of them. They both love to sunbathe, Leo especially, which surprises me because I would think a Husky is miserable in the hot sun, but he loves it.

"They sunbathed for a few hours today, you know how they love it," Kait says to me. "We've been waiting for you to get home so we can go dump the motorhome. I was thinking we could take the boys and let them ride in it for the first time."

"Sounds good to me. We'll need to pack up before we can head out."

Walking in to the motorhome, I realize that getting it ready to drive is going to take some time. It looks like an explosion went off in here. There's stuff all over the place so I start with a white box full of paperwork Kait has open on the table. "Where does this go?"

"Over there," she says pointing to one of the drawers in the pantry.

I grab a few other things and inquire as to where she would like them but she gets frustrated and says, "It would be a lot faster if you let me take care of this. Why don't you take the boys for a nice long walk and I'll have everything put away by the time you get back."

I can't argue with that. I leash up the boys and we head out on our nightly walk. It's been in the 90s during the day but gets nice and cool in the evening. With the windows open and the two roof fans running, we've managed to keep the motorhome cool enough so we don't have to run the A/C. The closets are another story. Heat from the walls seems to get trapped in them and when we open them, it feels like opening the door to a sauna.

Duke and Leo have had no problems hanging out and sleeping in the motorhome, but I'm not sure how they will react once their new home starts moving. I don't think they'll have any problems with it, but one of Leo's favorite places to sleep is under the steering wheel. He can't be under there while I am driving. A few nights ago we both got woken up by this loud mechanical noise and saw red flashes coming from the rear of the motorhome. Half asleep, we panicked thinking it was on fire or something had happened. Turns out Leo rolled over onto the brake pedal in the middle of the night. The noise was the electric brake system and the light was the bright LED brake lights flashing on and off as Leo rolled on and off the pedal. We had a good laugh that night once we realized what happened.

Kait is waiting for the three of us when we get back from the walk and has everything put away. "I don't know how you do it babe," I say. It looks spotless in here and everything has found a home in a cabinet or a drawer.

"The boys will ride with you and I'll follow in the Jeep."

"Are you guys good with that?" I ask the boys who are staring back at me like I have a treat for them. "I'll take that as a yes. Let's bring the slides in and leveling jacks up, then we'll be ready to go. By the way, where are we going?"

"You know the gas station over on Sherman Way? They have a dump station there and it's less than a mile away."

"Perfect. A short drive will be good for the boys' first adventure in our new home."

To bring the slide in, Kait repositions the carpets while I rotate the two front seats into the driving position. The big slide comes in first followed by the bedroom slide. My worries about the new bed not fitting under the closets are alleviated when I see the mattress slide under the closets without any problem.

"Bud, you have to move. You can't lay there when I'm driving." Leo looks up at me like I'm crazy and lays his head back down. I reach down to give him a nudge and although he's reluctant, he finally decides that he'd rather move than have me poking him. After he's out from under the steering wheel, he jumps up on the couch with a "don't bother me again" look. Duke is lying on his bed, which Kait relocated right between the two front seats.

I start the engine and press the button to retract the hydraulic jacks. The motorhome starts coming down to rest its full weight on the tires. "Don't worry guys, we're just going for a short drive." They know something is up. Duke is standing on his bed and Leo has jumped off the couch and positioned himself next to Duke. I take the parking brake off, put the motorhome in drive and start to move down the driveway slowly. The boys look a bit nervous, but so far so good. I continue down our street at a slow pace to avoid the trees and help the boys get used to the fact that their new house is now moving. Times like this, I wish I knew what they were thinking.

As we turn the corner onto the main street, a few of the kitchen drawers fly open. Both boys panic and before I can react, Leo pushes his way under my legs and Duke jumps in my lap. There are cars parked along this entire side of the street and I need to pull over, but I don't see any place to stop. I'm trying to keep the motorhome straight, but every little sway sends the drawers flying and Duke further into my lap. At this point he's completely blocking me from reaching down to keep Leo from leaning on the gas or brake pedal. Luckily, I nudge Leo over a bit with my right leg and I reach the brake pedal. I don't see anywhere to stop so I put my hazards on and stop in the middle of the road.

"Duke, off!" He doesn't move and I have to lift him off my lap and run back to close all the drawers. This is the second time this has happened. We need some sort of checklist to go through before we get on the road.

Out of the corner of my eye, I see Kait running up to the door.

"Everything okay?" She yells into the motorhome.

"No, all of the drawers flew open and the boys freaked out. Can you take them and put them in the Jeep? I can't drive with them in here."

Until this point, Leo was planted firmly under the steering wheel, but when he sees Kait reach for his leash, he springs towards her like he can't get out fast enough. This was a bad idea. We both should have been in here so I could focus on driving and Kait could manage the boys. We had no idea things would go this sideways. I just hope that the boys aren't traumatized by the whole experience.

We've created quite the traffic backup, but everyone is staying pretty calm. I don't know if it's the motorhome, but normally people would be honking and screaming at this point. Once Kait takes the boys and everything is secured, I put the motorhome back in drive and head towards the gas station. I'm surprised that this gas station has a dump. I assumed that only RV parks had dump stations and we would need to drive to one and pay a fee. When I pull into the station, I spot the RV dump along the back end of the building, away from the pumps. There is a pad lock on the sewer drain cover with a "Pay Cashier Inside" sign next to it. I try my best to line the motorhome up so our drain is next to the dump.

"Looks like we have to go inside and pay first," I say to Kait as she walks over. "Do you know how much it is?"

"It's $30 to dump but the next closest one, which costs $10, is 15 miles away. Since we get about 6 mpg in the motorhome and gas is over $3 per gallon, we'd spend almost as much to drive there and back."

"Good point. You watch the boys and I'll go in and pay."

I tell the clerk that I am there to dump my tanks and she takes out a clipboard. She has me fill out the make/model of the motorhome, license plate number and how many gallons I am dumping. Apparently it has to do with city record keeping. Once I have the paperwork filled out, I pay the clerk and she hands me the key to the pad lock.

Aside from the short tutorial that Jack gave us on how to dump the tanks, I've never dumped before. I have watched numerous videos on how to do this, but I also read the stories Kait found about things going wrong and someone ends up covered in waste. That's not a story I ever want to tell around a campfire. To help protect myself, I bought latex gloves and a plastic storage bin to store the sewer hose. I slip a pair of the gloves on and pull the hose out of the wet bay. The wet bay is where all the sewer connections are and the fresh water intake. Kait and the boys are standing a safe distance from the dump, no doubt waiting to see what happens. I connect one end of the sewer hose to the outlet on the motorhome and the other to the sewer drain. The hatch for the sewer drain has a lever on it that I step on to hold the hatch open as I slip the sewer hose nozzle into the drain. Maybe sandals weren't the best choice of footwear for this job.

I squat down and find the levers for the gray and black tanks. I pull the lever for the black tank first and in a second I can see the contents flowing through the sewer hose's clear elbow. I didn't think too much about it, but having the clear elbow will be helpful to know when everything is finished flowing out of the tank. I get a whiff of what's draining into the sewer and it's bad, but I'd much rather deal with this than the bucket toilet.

"Oh my God that smells horrible!" Kait says.

"Imagine what it smells like for me!" I yell back at her.

"Imagine what it smells like for the boys!" Kait yells back and we both laugh.

As the black tank continues to empty, I grab a small hose I picked up for this occasion and hook it up to the gas station's water spigot and the other end to our black tank flush valve. There are sprayers inside the black tank that will hose down the inside and help loosen any solid waste that is stuck.

About 30 seconds after turning on the hose, I see a few good sized chunks float past the clear elbow and let the sprayers run until everything flowing out is clear. We are the only RV in line at the dump station, so I don't feel guilty about taking time to thoroughly flush the black tank. Plus, we just paid $30 to dump the tanks so I'll spend as much time as I need to get the job done. Apparently, if there's a line of RVs waiting to dump, it's common courtesy to try and speed up the process.

With the black tank flushed, I close the valve and open the valve for the gray tank. True to its name, the water that comes out is gray and somehow smells worse than the waste from the black tank. The water has been sitting in that tank since we bought the motorhome. With the hot weather, my guess is that it's been fermenting. I make a mental note to dump the tanks more often so we don't have to deal with that smell again and to look into some sort of tank treatment.

Half an hour later, I can finally say that I've managed to dump our tanks without getting crap all over me. The last thing I wanted was to relive that scene in *RV* with Robin Williams. It's a proud moment and looking back at Kait, she's clearly relieved.

"Hey babe, I'm starving," I tell Kait. "What do you want to do for dinner?"

"How can you think about food after that?"

"You know me," I say with a wink as I pull off my latex gloves, tossing them into the dumpster.

Kait laughs and nods her head. "I'm hungry too, I just didn't think you'd want to eat anything after that. Do you want me to go pick up some Chinese takeout?"

"That'd be great. I can drive the motorhome back and get it in the driveway while you and the boys go get us some food."

"Will you be good to park it back in the driveway without me?"

"I should be fine. If I have any problems, I'll wait for you to get home."

"Please be careful and wait for me to get back with the food. We can eat in the house and then get the motorhome back in the driveway."

"Hurry home, I'm starving!"

21. PARTY FAVORS

Wednesday, July 15th, 2015

"Hey John, this is Joe."

"Hey Joe, how's the house coming along?"

"That's exactly why I'm calling. The yard looks great and I've finished most of the painting and other work that needed to get done. The only thing we have left is to get everything out of the house."

"When do you think you can get that done? I have some paperwork I need you to sign before I can list the house and I'll need to take some photos."

"Let's see. It's Wednesday so why don't we plan for you to come over next Monday to take pictures and we can sign the documents."

"See you on Monday then. Thanks Joe, talk to you later."

We've been making progress on the house, but there is still a lot of stuff left for us to go through. I never realized how much we had until we started emptying the closets, cabinets and anywhere else we stashed things. We've sold or given away most of our furniture, but there are still some large items left. Most of our other things have been listed for sale, but anything we can't sell, donate or giveaway will have to be thrown out. There is too much to go through and not enough time.

"Hey babe, I'm home!" I yell as the dogs try their best to knock me over.

"Hey honey, how was your day?"

"Eh, nothing special. I did talk to John today and he's going to come over this coming Monday to take pictures and get the house listed. We'll need to clear the rest of this stuff out of here by then."

"Monday? I think we need more time than that, don't you? And when are you going to work on selling your motorcycles?"

"The garage is pretty empty now. I figured we could sell some more stuff and take more to the donation center. What we can't sell or donate, we can move into the garage until we close on the house. This will at least give us time to go through anything that's left and figure out what we want to load in the motorhome."

"I have a great idea," Kait says as she jumps off the couch. "Let's have a party this weekend. We can tell everyone who comes that they have to take something home with them. There are some nice things left so it should be a win-win for everyone."

"I like it. You work on inviting friends to the party and I'll be working on getting more stuff sold."

"Don't forget about the motorcycles."

"Yes dear," I say with a smirk.

I've spent almost every lunch break for the last two weeks either in meetings or going to the post office to ship something I sold on eBay. Many of the items are lightly used and have been sitting around collecting dust. I sold my other motorcycles pretty quickly, but the Suzuki is going to be hard to let go. I took my last ride on her this past weekend and got some great shots for my classified ad. I've been putting off listing it, but it's finally time to part with her. We had some fun adventures together in the past six years. Kait still likes to joke about the fact that my last road trip entailed riding through the desert in 100 degree weather with my full leather gear on. Despite the heat, that was one of my fondest memories on this motorcycle.

After our nightly walk with the boys, I list more items for sale, including the Suzuki. Duke seems to sense my mood and makes his way over to cuddle around my feet. After about an hour, I think my left leg has fallen asleep, but so has Duke and I stay still so I don't wake him. The smaller items that I can easily ship are being listed on eBay, and the larger items like the motorcycle end up on Craigslist. The nice thing about Craigslist is there are no fees and the buyers pay in cash. The bad part is that I never know what type of people I'll be dealing with. There's the person who wants to buy everything at half the asking price and precedes every encounter with "I give you good price." The flakes are the worst. People will set up a time to meet and never show up or arrive an hour late and wonder why I'm not there waiting for them. After everything has been listed, I wake Duke and we both head into the bedroom. Kait's been asleep for about an hour. It dawns on me that with the small quarters in the motorhome, if I am going to be on the laptop or watching TV while she's sleeping, I'm going to need a good pair of headphones.

Kait has been working from home all week, getting things organized and put away whenever she takes a break. After I came home the last few nights, she's had piles of stuff for me to go through. What I don't want to keep is taken to the donation center while the rest gets moved into the garage. I had to veto a few of the items that Kait wanted to toss. Some I want to keep to see if we have room for them in the motorhome, and others I can sell or give to friends. One of the hardest things for me to get rid of, besides the motorcycle, are clothes. The first pass was easy, pick out all the clothes that don't fit or are worn out. The next pass is more difficult because these are clothes I wear occasionally. I like these clothes, but unless I wear them on a regular basis, it doesn't make sense to keep them.

"Kait, can you come in here and help me? I need your opinion on what to keep and what to donate."

"Sure, be right there," Kait says and appears in the doorway to the walk-in closet. She studies my side of the closet and then looks back at me. "So you're getting rid of all that?"

"That's what I need your help with. These are the clothes I wear occasionally and I'm trying to decide what to keep and what to get rid of. I'm having a hard time because some of these clothes are nice and I may need them one day."

"Okay," Kait says shaking her head. She's embraced the minimalist lifestyle much better than I have. To be honest, I am struggling and Kait's "get rid of everything" motto is starting to frustrate me. Kait begins flipping through everything I have hanging in the closet and pulling out seemingly random articles of clothing. "Donate all of these," she says pointing to the pile she's made. "These don't look good on you."

"That was easy. What's next?" I ask.

"Strip and start trying everything on. I'll give you a yes or a no."

I take my clothes off as ordered and start to try things on. The "nos" are coming a lot more often than the "yeses," but I feel like we're making progress.

"Let's go through the drawers next," I tell Kait.

Most of the stuff ends up in the donation pile except for a few sweaters and my hiking gear. We both hope to spend more time outdoors with the boys once we get on the road.

"What's next?" Kait asks.

I scan the bedroom and the closet one last time and turn back to her. "Nothing. Thanks, that was helpful. I think the keep pile is small enough that I might be able to find room for most of it."

"Great, happy to help. If you need me to help you get rid of more stuff, just let me know," Kait says as she walks out of the bedroom and on to her next project. I get the sense that Kait is fully in her element now. I don't think I've seen her quite as happy as she is when she's getting rid of stuff.

The "take something home with you" party is tomorrow. I head into the living room and find Kait making more piles, this time for guests to take. They're all nice things that we would keep if we had the room. There are wine aerators, stemmed and stemless wine glasses, candle holders, book ends, plates, board games, the list goes on.

I never knew this, but the donation centers can be quite picky about what they take. Kait has come home with a number of bags that they wouldn't take and promptly got tossed in the garbage. Lucky for us, one of our neighbors is in the process of renovating their house and rented a huge dumpster. They told us we were welcome to use it so we've been tossing all sorts of stuff in there, including the bucket toilet. I thought for a second about trying to give it away, but I can't imagine anyone would be interested, "Free homemade bucket toilet, only used for a few weeks."

What's not in Kait's giveaway pile I take into the garage to organize into my own piles. One for things we're trying to sell, another for things going into the motorhome and another for things I'm still not sure about. It's a small two-car garage and by the time I am finished, it's so full, I can hardly walk from one end to the other.

We work through most of the evening and by midnight the house is almost empty. "I scheduled a cleaning crew to come on Sunday and go through the house," Kait says as I walk back in the motorhome after locking up the garage.

"That's a great idea. I'm wiped out from all of the painting and it would be great to have someone else come in and clean. I've been dreading that part."

"I figured you were. Plus I thought it would be a nice break, we both need it."

Kait scheduled the party to start at 3 p.m. so we could grill in the backyard and use the outdoor furniture we haven't sold yet. With the house empty, we have no place to sit inside. She gave everyone strict instructions not to bring anything as we have plenty to drink and enough food for everyone. Having people over made me think of the bucket toilet and what the conversation would have been if a friend needed to go in and use it. I shake my head and chuckle.

Around 3 p.m., people start trickling in and by 4:30 the backyard is filled with some of our closest friends. I have the grill going with the standard fare along with some marinated meats we picked up at the local Korean market. Kait is busy making drinks for everyone. It's been a fun evening and turned into a kind of going away party. We may not have time to get together with some of these friends again. It was nice to take a break from getting the house ready to sell and moving into the motorhome. The stress of trying to get our lives ready for this huge change has been draining on both of us. I've told a few close friends I trust at work about our plans, but otherwise people at work are clueless. Kait has been doing the same with her co-workers. We've had to be careful with what we post on social media and we always have to be careful about what we say at work so as not to set off any alarms. Everyone at the party knows about our plans so it has been fun to let loose and give everyone a tour of our new home.

Most of our friends are in awe of what we've planned to do. The most common statement is, "I wish I could do that." Everyone has their reasons why they can't and it makes me think back to when Kait first came up with the idea. When she told me, I immediately thought of all the reasons why we couldn't do it rather than all of the ways we could make it work. Taking a risk like this required me to rethink a lot of the social norms that have been drilled into us by society. Friends of ours in finance think we're crazy to be giving up great careers and selling the house for a life of no income and living out of a depreciating asset. They don't understand that we've changed our mentality and making a six-figure income no longer drives how we live our lives. Happy, healthy, together and with the world as our backyard, that's how we want to live.

As people begin to leave, we try to hand off as many "party favors" as we can. A few picked through Kait's pile of stuff right from the beginning, but everyone else seems like they're simply taking something out of charity. At least it won't take up space in our garbage can.

"People stayed a lot longer than I expected," Kait says.

It's midnight and the last of our guests left about twenty minutes ago. "I was surprised too. It was a lot of fun, but people didn't take nearly as much stuff as I had hoped. Do you want to try and take what's left down to the donation center tomorrow?"

"Sure, we can take care of that in the morning. I'm ready for bed, coming?"

Sunday morning, I wake up to an email from a guy who's interested in the Suzuki. That's perfect because we'll be home most of the day with the cleaning crew working on the house. Still in bed, I email the guy back to tell him I'm free and give him the address. Kait climbs out of bed and heads into the house to meet the cleaning crew and I sneak in a few extra minutes of snooze time. With our schedule lately, I haven't been able to sleep in for a long time and I miss it. I may not be able to take "real" showers once we're on the road, but I can't wait for the day I no longer have to set an alarm.

At noon, a car pulls up to the house and two guys walk over. "Hey are you Joe?" the younger man asks as they approach.

"I am, are you Adam?"

"Yep, and this is my dad Frank."

"Nice to meet you," I say shaking their hands. "The bike is in the garage, let me pull it out so you can get a better look at it."

I walk back into the garage and start snaking the Suzuki between boxes and around the motorhome. There's not much room, but I make it work.

"Do you have a bike now?" I hear Kait ask Adam.

"No, I don't. I've wanted one for a while. Just passed the motorcycle course and got my license. I've read great things about the Suzuki and this one looks like it's in great shape."

"Yeah, Joe took great care of the bike."

Kait's right, even though I've had her for five years and put on over 40K miles, she still looks new.

"Okay, here she is," I say pulling the bike out to the front of the driveway.

Adam looks the bike over, sits down on it and plays around with the controls. "Do you mind if I start it?" He asks.

"Not at all, here's the key."

Adam loves the bike and we come to an agreement on the price. Once all the paperwork is done, he grabs his motorcycle gear from the car.

"I'm a bit nervous. Aside from the little bikes we rode in class, this will be my first time riding my own bike," Adam admits.

"Well, don't rush and take some time to get used to it. How far do you have to go?"

"I live about 60 miles from here. I figure I'll take surface streets home. I don't feel comfortable getting on the highway yet."

Now I feel scared for my poor bike. I can't say it's mine anymore, but I just hope he makes it home in one piece.

"Good luck and be careful. Nice to meet you, Adam."

With all of his gear on, Adam puts the bike in gear and stalls it as he tries to ride away. He starts it up again and this time he over revs the engine, almost falling off as he pulls away from the house. Watching him ride off, he looks like a kid riding a bicycle after they realize their dad has let go of the seat.

"That was hard to watch," I say turning back to Kait.

"I know, but now it's one less thing to worry about and I'm sure this won't be your last motorcycle."

A few hours later, the cleaning crew is done and we take a look through the house.

"I think we should have hired a cleaning crew sooner," I say. "They did a great job, the house looks so much better."

"It does. I'll be curious to see what John thinks when he comes over tomorrow."

22. FOR SALE

Monday, July 20th, 2015

John gets to the house not long after I get home from work. Kait heads out to greet him while I finish changing and come out with the boys.

"Hey John, good to see you," I say.

"I was just telling Kait that the house looks great. I'm impressed with what you did with the yard. There is definite curb appeal and that's going to draw people in. More importantly, I'm impressed with the motorhome you bought. I know you guys have a lot going on so let me take some pictures while there's still light and then we can sit down and go through the paperwork."

I make a pot of coffee while John is taking pictures and when he's done, we all sit down to go over the paperwork. Duke is at John's feet getting the back of his ears scratched while Leo is lying next to Kait. We go through all of the paperwork that needs to be signed and John explains the process of selling the house. With the house cleaned and emptied, John plans to hold a brokers open house this week followed by a general open house on Saturday and Sunday.

"Do we need to move the motorhome for the open house?" Kait asks.

"I don't see any problem with leaving it. It looks great and will give people an idea of how big your driveway is. You'd be surprised how many buyers I meet who are looking for a house that has enough property to park an RV. I do however recommend that the two of you aren't here during the open house. If you give me a key, I will get here around 10 a.m. to get the house set up and I'll plan to end the showing around 3 or 4 p.m. depending on what the foot traffic is like."

"How long do you think it will take to sell the house?" I ask.

"There are a lot of factors, but I don't think it's going to take long to go into escrow. The nicer properties in this area have gone into escrow within two weeks and I wouldn't be surprised if you end up getting multiple offers. The house will be on MLS tomorrow and I'll email you a link once it's up."

The merger at work still hasn't gone through, but I'm working more with teams from the other company so I get the feeling that it should be completed soon. Kait is headed to New York tomorrow for work and it will be the first time the boys and I have the motorhome to ourselves.

One to-do I've had hanging over my head is the Jeep. I still need to get it set it up for towing behind the motorhome. Most people do this by installing a baseplate onto the Jeep which connects the Jeep to the tow bar from the motorhome. We decided to get a heavy-duty off-road bumper that has special mounting points for the tow bar rather than getting a baseplate.

The Jeep also needs a system installed that, when the Jeep is being towed and the motorhome's brakes are applied, applies the Jeep's brakes. There are many systems out there and we chose the ReadyBrute Elite. It's a combination tow bar and braking system that uses the inertia of the Jeep pushing against the motorhome to activate a mechanical lever that, in turn, pulls a cable that applies the Jeep's brakes. We like the simplicity of the mechanical system compared to some of the more complex and expensive systems.

My concern now is that I ordered all of the parts a month ago and still don't have them. The bumper is made to order and has to be specially shipped because of its size. The tow bar is back ordered and the estimated delivery date is the end of July. It shouldn't take more than a day or two for me to install everything, but I would like to have access to the garage when I do it.

While Kait's in New York, I work on organizing everything I am taking and pack it into the bays of the motorhome. One thing I need to keep in mind as I am storing things, is to try and balance the weight as best as I can. This is important so I don't overload one side and cause a potential safety issue. The first bay on the driver's side is where our 20-gallon propane tank lives and next to that is a large bay that's perfect for all my tools. I have a large Nantucket Bag for easy access to many of my everyday tools along with a smaller Craftsman tool box that I load in the bay. I find a spot for my Dremel and power drill and toss in our hatchet and folding shovel. I have always kept small bags of things like nuts, bolts and washers and throw a couple of those in there too, never know when I'll need them.

The "tool bay" as I am now calling it looks good and I move on to the wet bay. It has two doors, one to access the sewer connections and a larger door to access the water inlet and outdoor shower. I have the sewer and tank flush hoses stored in there with a box of latex gloves, a roll of paper towels and a container of disinfectant wipes to clean things off after we dump the tanks. I really mean "I" because I don't expect that Kait is going to do much dumping while we're on the road. I decided to leave the fresh water hose out of this bay because I don't want it touching anything that is involved with the dumping process.

Past the rear wheels, there is a smaller bay with a chamber that goes back to about the center of the motorhome. The strange thing is that the chamber is not too tall and there is no way to reach the back of it. I'd need a stick or something to get back there. I have no idea what to store in here. Best to leave it empty for now and see if Kait can come up with a use for it.

The last bay on the driver's side is one of the largest. It's called a "pass through" because the bay goes clear through with a door on the other side. This is going to be great for longer items. The 30 amp electric cord for the motorhome is housed in this bay. When it's coiled up, the cord doesn't take up too much space and gives me plenty of room for the fresh water hose, portable EMS and other items we need to set up camp.

The other side of this pass through bay is the rear passenger side of the motorhome and is taller than the other side. I load all the cleaning supplies into an old crate for easy access and put it in the bay. The small suitcases we packed with our winter gear also gets stowed in here. The pass through area is perfect for our two long camp chairs and small folding table.

Moving toward the front of the motorhome, the next bay houses the 4kW Onan generator. Past that are the rear wheels followed by three more bays. The first two are wide but not very deep. One is obscured by the black tank and the other by the fresh water tank. I move our camp stove, canned food and gallon water bottles into the first of these bays. The next is the perfect size for the dogs' 40 pound airtight food container. The last bay, next to the entrance of the motorhome, is deep and narrow. I stick the broom in there and a pair of tree branch cutters. If we ever run across branches that are in the way, one of us can get on the roof and cut them down. This will also be a good place to store all of our shoes. The steps into the motorhome are next to the shoe bay and can double as a seat for taking shoes off and putting them back on.

As much stuff as I have moved into the motorhome, it looks like I've barely made a dent in the garage. The piles don't appear to be getting any smaller so I start sifting through each one and throwing out anything we don't want, can't donate or isn't worth selling. There are a few things like an old lamp, box fans and left over copper pipe that I put by the curb for people to pick up. Our neighborhood has several scrap metal collectors who will drive around the night before trash day and pick up things like this. Tools like my circular saw and belt sander will go to my brother-in-law who does a lot of home improvement work.

After a few hours of working in the garage, the boys start nudging me to take them for another walk which makes a great excuse to call it a night. The garbage can is full, and it looks like I've made a noticeable dent. There are a few things I put aside for Kait to go through when she gets home, but this was time well spent and I'm feeling a little less overwhelmed.

When I get back from the walk, there is a voicemail from John. "Hi Joe, this is John. We had the broker's open today and it went well. I heard from one of the brokers that we should be getting an offer in a day or two. I'm also having the general open house this weekend and will be there around nine in the morning. Don't worry about calling me back, we can speak on Saturday. Have a great night."

"That's great news and I needed that today," I think to myself. I've been quite stressed lately with getting the house ready to sell, the pending merger at work, trying to move into the motorhome and planning our new life. When we first came up with the idea of traveling around the country in a motorhome, It seemed so simple. Buy a motorhome, sell the house and quit our jobs. Easy peasy. What started as a simple idea has become one of the most involved projects that I've ever undertaken. We're taking a huge risk and completely changing the direction of our lives. Trying not to forget anything and cover all of our bases is frightening at times. I've wondered if we're doing the right thing more than once.

It feels like I am standing on the edge of a cliff, about to leap off into the unknown. We've planned for over a year now and hopefully we will soar rather than sink when we make that jump into the unknown. Only time will tell.

For the past week, Duke has spent his time staring out the front of the motorhome watching our street, waiting for Kait to come home from her trip. He used to do the same thing when we lived in the house. If either of us was gone, Duke would go to his post and only leave it to eat, walk or sleep. Leo on the other hand is a true Husky. He acts like he could care less about what's going on as long as there is someone around to feed him. I know Leo's act is all a show because as soon as Duke alerts us that Kait is driving down the street, Leo is up and just as excited as Duke and I are.

"Hey babe, welcome home!" I say walking over to the driver's side door of her Honda Civic. "Want to pop the trunk so I can grab your bags?"

"Thank you honey. It's been a long few days and I couldn't wait to get home to you and the boys."

"Well Duke's been doing his thing at the front window and they are both inside waiting for you."

When Kait opens the door to the motorhome the boys almost knock her down, each trying to be the first to greet her. "It's so good to be home. Feels weird saying that in the motorhome, but I guess this is home now."

"Are you going into the office tomorrow?" I ask.

"No, I am taking tomorrow off so it will be a nice three day weekend. I know we've both been stressed lately and I was thinking that maybe we could take the motorhome on a mini vacation this weekend. It would be a good chance to practice living in it before we hit the road. Most camp-grounds within an hour from here are all booked this week-end, but there are a couple right along the ocean that are first-come, first-served. What do you think?"

"I think it's a great idea. Would we drive up there and see if we get lucky finding an open spot?"

"Pretty much. I have a few places marked on the map that we can check out. Worst case scenario, park by the beach for the afternoon and drive back that evening."

"I have to be at work tomorrow so do you want to go up Saturday morning?"

"That's what I was thinking. We can go early in the morning and hopefully find a spot. Okay honey, I'm heading to bed, love you." Kait is asleep when her head hits the pillow and the boys join her on their respective beds. I can tell that Duke, especially, is much more relaxed with Kait home.

When I get home from work Friday night, we start pack-ing some of the things I've piled up in the garage for our trip. A couple of days lounging at the beach is just what the doc-tor ordered and I'm trying not to get too excited. If all of the other campgrounds are full, why wouldn't the first-come, first-served places be as well? The saving grace might be that these spots are all dry camping. No facilities, just a large parking spot to accommodate an RV right along the beach. Hopefully they won't be as popular as the campgrounds with full hook-ups and all the amenities. With our first trip in the motorhome tomorrow, we head to bed once everything is packed.

23. BEACH FRONT PROPERTY

Saturday, July 25th, 2015

Kait's alarm goes off at 6 a.m. and we waste no time getting out of bed. I am getting the dogs leashed up for their morning walk while Kait starts working on getting the motorhome ready for us to hit the road. "Don't pack my coffee stuff. I want to make a cup for the road," I say as the boys drag me outside.

Although we don't have an official checklist, Kait and I go through the motorhome to make sure we didn't accidentally leave any drawers unlocked, windows open, or anything else that may fly open when we take that first turn. Once we're sure the motorhome is buttoned up, I hop in the driver's seat and get us off the jacks.

"Before we take off, I want to check the tires. I read we should check them before every trip," I tell Kait.

With motorhome tires, the PSI they are inflated to represents the load they can handle. At 110 PSI, the tires we have can carry their maximum stated load. Each tire manufacturer has tables that show what PSI to have the tires inflated to for the amount of weight they will be carrying. I have no idea how much the motorhome weighs with everything we've moved into it, but I do know what the PSI needs to be if the motorhome is unloaded. I want to make sure it's at least higher than that number until we have a chance to weigh the motorhome. After my checks, the PSI for most of the tires is lower than I want them to be.

"Let's stop at the gas station before we get on the freeway so we can air up the tires, we're a bit low all the way around."

We stop at the same gas station where we dumped a few weeks ago. I noticed their air pump is right next to the dump and it will be easy to get in and out of there. Pulling up to the pump I realize that there is no way to reach both sides unless I air up one side then drive out and come back in the opposite direction. I have no idea how long it will take to add the extra 10 PSI so I let the pump run for a minute and check the pressure multiple times because I don't quite believe what I am seeing. The pressure in the driver's side tire has actually gone down. I try to pump more air into the tire, but when I check the tire has lost more pressure. The pump doesn't appear to have the power to inflate tires this size.

"All done?" Kait asks when I come back in.

"No, this pump isn't powerful enough to inflate these tires. I actually lost two PSI. Can you see if there is a truck stop somewhere along our route where we can stop and get some air?"

"Sure, I'll check once we're on the freeway. I want to make sure the boys are calm and don't try jumping in your lap. We don't need a repeat of last time."

Aside from the short trips to the gas station, the only other time we've driven the motorhome was coming home from the dealership. It's a bit unnerving pulling onto the highway and getting up to 55 mph. The nice thing is that the roads are pretty empty this early on a Saturday and we have a straight shot up the 101 Freeway to the Ventura area.

"I don't see any truck stops along this stretch of 101," Kait informs me. "Do you want me to find another gas station we can try?"

"Sure, and maybe give them a call to ask if their pump is powerful enough to air up truck tires."

Kait finds another place about twenty minutes from where we are and they confirm over the phone that the pump is new and should have no problem with our big tires. As we get closer, I see the gas station and pull off. The lack of early morning traffic is proving very beneficial right now because I have a lot less room to maneuver in this station.

"This one doesn't work either," I tell Kait after trying to inflate the tires again. "At least this time I tried the front passenger tire so it's now even with the driver's side."

"So what are we going to do?" Kait asks.

"Keep going. Short of finding a truck stop, I doubt we'll find a pump that's up to the task of filling these tires. We should be fine to drive to Ventura and back. I'll figure something out in the meantime."

The rest of the drive is uneventful and I'm getting more comfortable behind the wheel. "The exit is going to be past Rincon Parkway so we should see it before we get off the freeway. Look, there it is!" Kait says, pointing to the endless stretch of RVs parked along the beach.

There are 127 RV parking spots parallel to the beach, and from what I can see, every spot is filled. I even see some RVs double parked and can only assume they are waiting for a spot to open. It's 9 a.m. as we exit the freeway and make the right onto Hobson Road. We're about a mile from the start of the parking area and I see other RVs coming down the exit behind us.

"If we don't find anything here there is another camping area further down the road," Kait tells me as she studies her phone. I recognize the look on her face. She's concerned we won't find a spot.

As we pass the first few RVs, I've got my fingers crossed that we find an open spot. The parking is situated on the ocean side of Hobson Road. If we find a spot, we'll be able to open our door and walk right out onto the beach. It seems like the only obstacle to the sand is a rocky breakwater that shouldn't be too hard to climb down. People are walking and biking along the long row of RVs, some even have tables and chairs set up on the street side of their RV to watch people go by.

"I don't think there are any open spots. Looks like all of the people double parked are waiting for others to vacate their spot so they can pull in," I say.

"Let's keep going, you never know. There are 127 spaces."

As we get closer to the end of the parking area, I spot a truck towing a fifth wheel pulling out of a spot. "There!" I say pointing to the vacated spot. There aren't any RVs ahead of us, but I can see three or four behind us looking for spots.

"Grab it before anyone else does!" Kait yells.

The boys look as excited as we are. They've been great the entire drive up to Ventura and it's no surprise that Leo was passed out for most of it. I think they just needed their mother to hold their paws and reassure them that nothing bad was going to happen. We are a pack and happiest when we're all together. It also helped that nothing flew open in the middle of this drive.

I put my turn signal on and pull alongside the space to let the other RVs behind me pass. This is my first attempt to parallel park the motorhome. There is a dumpster and pay station at the front of the spot which gives me another twenty feet of space to maneuver. Plus, I doubt anyone would be upset if I put another dent in the dumpster, an RV would be another matter entirely. Kait gets out of the motorhome to guide me into the spot but with the side mirrors and rear camera, I don't have any difficulty. I do however end up too far on the beach side of the spot giving us almost no room to put out the camping chairs.

"You're too far on this side," Kait says as she walks up to the passenger's side of the spot.

"I know. How far over do I need to move?"

"If you can get your wheels to this point," Kait says making a mark on the pavement with her shoe, "then you should be perfect."

Looking in my side view mirror, I can see the driver's side rear wheels so I pull far enough over to line up the wheels with Kait's mark and back further into the spot. "How's that?" I yell.

"Looks good."

"Do we have enough room to put the big slide out?"

"Oh sorry, I forgot about that. You're going to have to move about a foot closer to the beach otherwise the slide will be blocking the bike path."

I do my little dance with the motorhome again and get it about a foot over to the beach side and back up to the very end of the spot so we have a good 10 feet of room in front of the motorhome. It's more than enough room to park the Jeep if we brought it. Kait returns to the motorhome and unlocks the slides so we can put them out and get the motorhome level.

"You want to get things set up?" I say leashing the boys up. "They need to stretch their legs and go to the bathroom so we can be out of your way."

"Sure. It will be easier to set up without the boys in here. Run along you three and have fun, I'll take care of this," Kait says pointing back into the motorhome.

On the opposite side of the road, there is a narrow strip of dirt along the shoulder where the boys relieve themselves. As we walk, they stop every few feet so they can smell the new scents. Duke and Leo love to explore and it puts a smile on my face thinking about all the new places they'll get to visit. As we slowly trot along, I'm marveling at the other campers' set ups. It looks like some people brought every comfort from home and I can't tell if they plan to stay for a month or the weekend. I'm impressed and a bit jealous. All we have are two camping chairs and two beach towels for the boys to lie on. Simple, but effective. Just the way we plan to live our new lives.

When we get back to the motorhome, Kait is finished and the boys run inside to fill up on water. I close the screen door behind them and leave the main door open to let the ocean breeze inside. It's a warm day, but with the breeze it feels great. The camping chairs are set up to face the ocean and I lay out the towels for the boys.

I've never had my own ocean front property before. This is pretty awesome. Looking over to my left, I see the pay station and realize we still need to pay for the spot. Surprised that there is an option to pay online, I plop down into one of the chairs and pull my phone and credit card out to pay for our stay.

"Honey, would you like a beer or a cocktail?" Kait asks from the kitchen window.

"Uh babe, it's still morning. Little early for a cocktail, wouldn't you say?"

"Why does it feel so much later? Maybe it's because we got up so early?"

"Just come out here and sit with me and the boys. Relax for a few minutes."

"I'll be out in a moment. Do you want me to put the awning out?"

"That's a good idea, it's hot in the sun and I don't want to burn. Actually, can you bring my hat out with you?"

We spend a few hours relaxing next to the motorhome in our camping chairs. The drive wore Leo out and he is passed out under the motorhome in the shade. Duke, on the other hand, has made it his mission to bark at every dog that walks by. He's always been very aggressive toward other dogs but took to Leo well. We've done extensive training with Duke, and he's gotten a bit better. However, in the past year, Duke's aggression towards other dogs has gotten worse. We will have to be careful camping around people with dogs.

"Do you want to take a walk along the beach?" Kait asks.

"I'd love to, let me grab some poop bags for the boys and we can take off."

The spot we're in has a trail down to the sand that seems to have been built up over the years by fellow campers. Neither of the dogs has any problems making it down, but I manage to slip and catch myself before hitting the rocks.

It is a perfect day. It's in the mid-80s with a blue sky and nice breeze off the water. There are families gathered along the beach with their children, others are running with their dogs and some even set up camp on the sand. Not a bad way to extend their "backyard."

Duke is dragging me down the beach. He's never been on the sand and loves it. Both of the boys are a little leery of the ocean, but as the surf comes up to my feet, Duke doesn't hesitate to follow me in. I keep walking until the water is around my knees. Growing up, we always had Labradors and they would go bonkers every time I took them near the water. Duke and Leo are the complete opposite. The only reason Duke is even in the water is because I'm in it. He would follow me anywhere. Duke's loyalty is on a level that I've never experienced with a dog before.

"Why don't you see if Leo will go in?" I ask.

"You take him. I don't feel like getting wet right now."

Kait and I exchange dogs and taking Leo by the leash, he follows me over to the water's edge. As soon as the surf touches Leo's front left paw, he bolts for dry sand. I've never seen him move that fast and he nearly pulls my arm out of the socket. At least now we know how Leo feels about the ocean.

At the end of the beach, we decide to find a way up the rock wall so we can walk back along the road. There is no space between each RV site so anywhere we walk up would put us in someone's campsite. Not only is this bad etiquette, according to the Park Ranger, it's also considered trespassing. We decide to look for campers outside to see if we can ask to walk through their site, otherwise we will walk back along the beach.

"Oww!" Kait yells, lifting up her right foot. "I just got stung by a bee."

"How'd that happen? Are you okay?"

"I must have stepped on it. I'm fine, but it hurts a lot."

"Hold still and give me your foot. I'll get the stinger out." I pull out my Benchmade folding knife and hold Kait's foot while I gently drag the edge of the blade along the bottom of her foot where she was stung. The stinger comes out, but I notice that she seems to be having a slight allergic reaction.

"Have you ever had an allergic reaction to bee stings?"

"I don't know. This is the first time I've been stung."

"It doesn't look too bad, but let's try and hurry back. Are you good to walk?"

"I think so."

As soon as I stand Kait up, we hear, "Do y'all need some help?" A woman and her husband are waving at us from their site at the top of the rocks.

"My wife got stung on the foot. Do you mind if we walk up through your site to get back to the road?"

"Absolutely not. By all means. Jim, go grab the Bactine so she can put some on her foot."

Kait is limping on her foot, but seems to be doing well. I'm a bit nervous because she has "Skeeter Syndrome" which causes her to swell up from mosquito bites. I'm hoping she doesn't have the same reaction, or worse, to bee stings. Jim and Mary have a few small dogs so I take the boys around the other side of their motorhome. Last thing I need is for Duke to go after one of them. Kait sits down in a folding chair that Mary grabbed, and Jim hands her a paper towel to clean her foot and then sprays a bit of Bactine on it. As the three of them are chatting, I walk the boys over to the other side of the road to see if they need to do their business and Kait joins us a few minutes later.

"How is your foot?"

"Much better. It still hurts to walk on it, but I don't think I am having any sort of reaction to the bee sting. Let's head back and I'll get lunch started."

As we walk down the row of RVs, Kait and I examine each one. It's amazing how many different types, sizes and shapes there are. Most people have motorhomes, but some have fifth wheels, small trailers, camper vans and some even appear to be living out of their cars. Most people look like regulars that come out for the weekend to get away from city life and spend a few days by the beach. I have a feeling this place gets rowdy on Friday nights.

The way people have decorated their sites is about as diverse as the RVs. There are huge outdoor seating areas, tables, BBQs, fencing for dogs and even games set up. We even spot one with a full Tiki bar. I have no idea how people get all this stuff up here. Not to mention the time to set it up for the weekend and to tear it all down again.

"Hey babe, check this out," I say to Kait as we walk by an older motorhome that has a solar panel propped up next to it.

"Oh interesting. I wonder if they bought the panels like that or if they made the stand?"

"Checkin' out the solar panel?" A guy asks as he comes around the motorhome.

"We are," Kait responds. "We're considering solar on the roof of our motorhome, but I like the set up you have. Did you make this yourself?"

"No, it's a 100 watt portable folding solar panel. The company who makes it is Renogy. I got it so we didn't have to run the generator as much when we come out here. It works great and I can move it to follow the sun. Plus it folds down and I store it in my rear bay."

Bob spends some time chatting with us about his solar unit and how he hooked it up to the motorhome batteries. We also learn that a group of retired police and firemen have "reserved" the nicer area of Rincon Parkway. The group has a schedule of who's camping in each spot and for how long.

Before one RV pulls away, the next one on the schedule will show up to take over the spot. I guess that explains all of the double parked RVs we saw earlier. Bob is a retired fireman and he and his wife were invited to be a part of the group but they aren't sure if they can make the commitment.

"So you're telling me you guys came up this morning and got a spot?" Bob asks and I respond with a nod. "You two won the lottery! I've never seen open spots on a Saturday, especially in the summer. If you come during the week you'll find something, but you have to be here by Thursday morning at the latest if you want to camp through the weekend."

Bob gives us a few more tips for our next trip and we say our goodbyes to head back to the motorhome for a late lunch. Kait makes one of my favorite meals. Gluten free Belgian waffles, eggs sunny side up and hot Italian sausages smothered in pure maple syrup and I make coffee to go with it. Life can't get much better than this moment. After lunch, we decide to stay in and relax. We got enough sun for the day and it's pleasant to sit inside listening to the waves crash. The boys are passed out on their beds, and we decide to follow suit and nap for a while.

Lying in bed, I decide to find a solution to our tire pump problem. I don't want to rely on truck stops to inflate the tires. In my search, I find that other RVers have run into the same type of problem. Some resorted to buying a cheap air compressor, but those are too big for us to carry. I end up finding a compact VIAIR compressor that is specifically made to air up large motorhome and truck tires. The reviews on it are great so I add it to my Amazon cart with a few other things we need. With that out of the way, I close my eyes, and the sound of the waves lull me to sleep.

It's 4 p.m. when we wake up from our nap. Neither of the boys felt like getting up so we leave them in the motorhome and head outside to enjoy the view. There are a handful of clouds in the sky and as the sun inches closer to the horizon, the colors over the water are brilliant.

"Would you like me to make you some coffee?" Kait asks.

"Sure, why not. It's starting to get a bit chilly so a hot cup of coffee would be great."

The sky goes from shades of orange and red to blue and gray as the sun drops below the horizon and night falls. The sunset made our fantastic view even more spectacular. "This has been one of the most relaxing days I've had in a long time," I tell Kait. "It's too bad we have to leave in the morning."

"If you want to stay longer we can always pay for another night. It would be nice to sleep in and not worry about rushing out of here. Plus, you can sit outside in the morning and have your coffee."

"Sold! I think that's a great idea."

24. GOT AN OFFER

We spend most of Sunday morning relaxing. I loved having my morning coffee while watching the waves crash without a worry in the world. When I'm by the ocean, I feel the most at peace. It's too bad we have to leave this slice of paradise. Now that I have a glimpse into our future life, I can't wait to get on the road full time. "It will all come together soon enough," I tell myself.

As I'm half way through my second cup of coffee, my phone starts buzzing. I'm tempted to ignore the call, but it's John and he's probably calling to discuss the open house. Last night I received an email from him with a recap of Saturday's activity. Seems like there was good traffic and several people expressed interest in our house. He expects more people to show up today.

"Hey John, what's up?"

"Joe, how's the beach?"

"Well I can't complain. I'm sitting here watching the waves break with a cup of coffee."

"That's good to hear, it seemed like the two of you needed a little time to recharge. I know this process can be stressful, but I have some news that should make things a bit better. We got an offer on the house today. One of the brokers that came to see the house last week brought her clients in today and they loved it. There are a few minor contingencies that we can walk through when you get back. Do you think you'll be available to meet tomorrow?"

"That is great news, thank you. We should be home by about 6 tomorrow evening so come over any time after that."

"Okay. I'll plan to be at the house by 6:30. I'll let you get back to your coffee. Bye."

As much as I would like to sit here and zone out with my coffee for another hour, I'm too excited about the news and head into the motorhome.

"Babe, John called and we got an offer on the house."

"That's fantastic! Did he say how much the offer was for?"

"No, I forgot to ask. He only said that there were some minor contingencies. He's going to come over tomorrow evening at 6:30 so we can go through it. Will you be home by then?"

"I was planning on working from home again so it won't be a problem. By the way, did you see that the bathroom sink is starting to separate from the counter?" Kait asks.

"No, let me take a look."

She leads me into the bathroom and sure enough there is a gap between the bottom of the sink and the counter.

"I'll add it to the list." We've been keeping track of issues with the motorhome that need to be addressed during the warranty period. "I'm going to call the service place on Monday and find out when we can bring the motorhome in. I would like to try to have it all taken care of before we hit the road full time. What time did you want to head home today?"

"I'd like to sit and watch the sunset with you again."

"I'd love that."

Shortly after 6:30 p.m., we decide to get everything packed up. Sunset will be in about an hour, and we can take off afterwards. While we've been here, Kait has been working on a checklist for us to go through each time we move the motorhome. Once we put everything away and bring in the slides, she pulls out her phone and starts reading off the list.

"Drawers closed?" She asks.

I check each drawer and shut two that are still ajar. "All the drawers are closed and locked."

"Everything in the bathroom put away?"

Checking the bathroom I confirm that nothing has been left out. It takes us about five minutes to go through the list, finding numerous things that we forgot to close or put away. Kait also adds a few items we need to check outside such as making sure all of the bay doors are closed and locked, the leveling blocks are put away and the tires are properly inflated. Once the motorhome is buttoned up and ready for the road, Kait grabs the camera and snaps a few pictures. We've been talking about getting our blog, weretherussos.com, up and running and Kait wants to write a post about our time at Rincon Parkway. After she's done taking photos, we find a place to sit on the rocks and enjoy the sunset together. The boys are unimpressed and promptly lay back down.

"I would like to drive home," Kait says as we head back into the motorhome.

"Are you sure? It's going to be dark on the way back."

"I need to start driving more so I can get used to it. You know I want to share the driving responsibilities. Since you drove us here, I want to drive us home."

"Sounds good to me. I can get a taste of what it's like to be a passenger in this thing."

Pulling out onto the road, Kait seems comfortable behind the wheel. I'm happy that I won't be doing all the driving. It will give me a chance to enjoy the scenery. The hour and a half drive here took a lot out of me because it was more work and concentration than driving a car. Whenever we passed a large truck, it felt like the gust of air coming off the truck might push us into the next lane. For most of the drive, I stayed in the right lane and cars were cutting us off left and right. It amazed me when a driver would cut in front of us and promptly slam on their brakes to make the exit. I guess they don't realize that our 22,000 pound motorhome can't slow down nearly as quickly as they can. I'm sure it will get easier over time, but right now I can't see spending hours behind the wheel.

The last daylight is finally gone as we merge on the freeway headed back towards Los Angeles. Out of my side window, I can see the dark ocean and the lights of numerous oil rigs in the distance. Kait has the cruise control set at 55 mph and we're quickly coming up on an old truck that is struggling to do 40. "I want to go around this guy, but I'm not sure if I can get over. I'm having a hard time gauging the traffic in the next lane."

The freeway is fairly busy with people headed home from their weekend getaway and cars are zipping by at 70 mph or faster. Few people respect the 65 mph speed limit, but trucks and anything towing a trailer must follow a slower 55 mph speed limit. Technically, we can drive 65 mph because we're not towing, but I know Kait is more comfortable at the lower speed. In the dark, the side view camera is almost useless with the headlights from other cars. This is making it hard to judge if Kait is clear to move into the next lane. I unbuckle my seat belt and lean on the couch to look out the window on the driver's side. "Okay, after this car you're clear," I say.

A sports car goes flying past and the lane is empty long enough for Kait to move over. I tell her to step on the gas to get around the old truck. We repeat this exercise every time Kait needs to switch lanes. It is going well, but I can tell Kait's nerves are on edge. It was a lot of work driving up here during the day, but twice as hard at night. Two hours later, we pull into the cul-de-sac and Kait breathes a huge sigh of relief.

"Do you mind backing the motorhome into the driveway?" Kait asks. "I'm not comfortable doing it in the dark. I can hop out and be your guide."

Getting the motorhome backed in is a different experience at night. Our street isn't well lit making it hard to find a reference point. It took me a few tries to get the motorhome in the driveway without hitting the curb. By the time I have the motorhome parked and leveled, it's after 10 p.m. and we're both wiped out. Once we're in bed, Kait looks over at me and says, "Let's not drive at night anymore, that wasn't fun."

The next day, John is at the house at 6:30 p.m. on the dot. We head into the guest bedroom where John has set up a makeshift office with three folding chairs and a folding table upon which he places all of the paperwork. I remember seeing some of these documents when we were house shopping. As much as I would love to have multiple offers, I don't look forward to the paperwork that goes along with each one.

"So their offer came in lower than what you wanted," John says. "My suggestion is to counter with something that you're comfortable with or you have the option of holding at your asking price."

"What were the contingencies you mentioned on the phone?" I ask.

"Well, they want to have the standard inspections done, but they also want to check to make sure things like the spa are in working order and that there aren't any problems with termites. They also mentioned they were interested in buying the washer, dryer and fridge from you."

"I'm happy to sell them the appliances, but I don't want to include them in the sale," Kait says.

"That's fine," John responds. "We can take care of the appliances separate from the house. Come up with a price you want for them and I'll pass it along to their agent."

The three of us continue discussing the terms of the offer and come up with a counter offer that we're happy with. Kait always insists on reading every page of a document she signs, so it takes a while to get through the stack.

When we bought this house, it probably took a few hours longer than normal to sign everything. I remember the escrow officer wasn't too happy about Kait reading every document and tried to rush us along, but we didn't care and studied every page before we signed. John knows us well and is happy to go through each page to make sure we understand everything and answer any questions.

"I'll present your offer to the buyer's agent in the morning and get back to you once I hear something. Have a great rest of your evening," John says as he packs up his briefcase.

Once John leaves, we take the boys on their nightly walk. The summer heat has been brutal during the day, but it cools down nicely in the evenings. It's the best time of the day to enjoy our walk around the neighborhood.

"Did you have a chance to call about our warranty issues today?" Kait asks as we round the corner onto the next street.

"Oh, I forgot to tell you. When I called about an appointment, the receptionist told me that they were completely booked until mid-September so I took the first appointment they had. Do you realize if the buyer accepts our offer, we'll be closing on the house at the end of August? Since the merger hasn't gone through yet, it means we may need to find an RV park to stay at for a few months."

"Let's worry about one thing at a time," Kait says. "We don't even know if our counter-offer will be accepted."

One of the reasons I love being with Kait is that she is very level headed when I start to get worked up. She helps to calm me down in these situations and I do the same for her. We complement each other well and it's one of the many reasons why I tell people that we'll have no problem living in such close quarters. Most of our family and friends have doubts and think we're crazy for doing this longer than a few months.

"You're right. I'm getting stressed about everything and it feels like there is always one more thing to worry about."

"I understand. Why don't we head back inside and relax for the rest of the night?"

On Wednesday, John calls to let us know our counter-offer was accepted and the clock has started for the 30-day escrow period. Given how busy this season is for home sales, John doesn't think the buyers will be able to get any appointments for inspections until next week. Our only stipulation is that John needs to be present whenever anyone is at the house. Although the house is empty, we have valuable things stored in the garage and we don't want anyone to accidentally break something. Plus, we want to make sure all the doors and the windows are locked after they leave. We don't live in the best neighborhood and there's no need to make things easy for a potential burglar.

25. PULLING THE TRIGGER

Friday, July 31st, 2015

True to John's word, we haven't seen any inspectors this week. I am up before the alarm goes off and sneak out of bed to keep from waking Kait and take the boys on their morning walk. She decided to work from home today because things have been crazy at the office and she hasn't been getting much sleep. After our walk, she's still sound asleep so I feed the boys and hop in the shower.

"Look who's finally awake!" I say walking into the bedroom after my shower.

"I might stay in bed all day," Kait says stretching. "I see you've got your coffee, are you leaving me?"

"Yep, time to go sit in traffic for my hour and a half commute. Although I have an interesting podcast to listen to today."

"Enjoy your podcast and we'll see you this evening. Hopefully you don't have to make this drive too much longer."

"You're telling me. Love you babe, bye!" I say giving Kait a kiss before I leave.

Getting into the Jeep, I place my coffee tumbler in the cup holder, lightly roasted almonds in the dash holder, and put on the podcast. This has been my morning routine for longer than I care to remember.

A few years ago I decided to make better use of the three hours that I spend in traffic each day. Rather than mindlessly listen to music or talk radio, I've found some great podcasts about history, permaculture, and building your own business. One of my favorites is The Survival Podcast, which is focused on making life better day to day by learning skills to make you more self-reliant. The topic I selected for today's drive is all about how to build a business and breaking free from the chains of corporate America. I'm particularly interested in hearing what Jack, the host, has to say on the subject. One thing I've been wondering about a lot lately is what we would do on the road for money if we decide to go for longer than one year.

By the time I pull into the parking lot at work, I feel inspired by the episode and start to brainstorm about how we can turn our new lifestyle into something that will allow us to continue indefinitely. We could continue to build our website, make videos about our adventure, start a podcast and even write a book.

Stepping out of the elevator, I know something is up. Everyone is huddled in groups talking amongst themselves. Admittedly I'm a bit late, but Friday mornings are usually slow. Today seems like an exception.

"What's going on?" I ask Jenny

"Didn't you check your email this morning?" She asks.

"No, I stopped doing that a few weeks ago. If anyone needs me badly enough, they can call."

I've been working with Jenny for over eight years and we've been through a lot together. At one point, most of our former department had either been fired or moved to another part of the company, but we managed to keep our little team together. Because of all this, Jenny is one of the few people in the office I truly trust. She is also in on my "secret."

I've been trying to include her in everything I work on so she can take over once I'm gone.

"The merger went through. They signed all the paperwork this morning and sent out a companywide email."

"No way!" I say jumping into my seat and opening Outlook. I see the email Jenny is referring to. Everything was approved this morning and the merger became official shortly after. "YESSSSS!" My inner voice is screaming with excitement. Stepping away from my desk, I find an unused conference room and shut the door.

"Babe, guess what?" I say on the phone to Kait. "The merger went through this morning. I should be able to put my notice in once I have my bonus check in hand."

"That's great news. I was starting to get a bit worried it wouldn't go through. How do you feel?"

"Relieved and excited. If all goes well, I should be getting my check about the same time we close on the house. It feels like things are starting to come together. Let's cross our fingers and hope everything goes smoothly with the sale of the house."

"It will," Kait assures me.

"I know. I better get back to my desk. It's past 10 and I have a few things that need to be taken care of this morning. Love you babe."

"Love you too, honey."

I haven't been this excited in a long time. Until I read the email, I felt chained to the company. Listing the house was a bit of a gamble. We agreed to wait until the merger was complete to get on the road. If we sold it before the merger was complete, we would need to find an RV park and live there until we could leave. Now, if all goes as planned, we should be on the road in a month or two.

When I get home that evening, we celebrate the good news by talking about the places we want to go and things we want to do. We haven't talked about it much because it didn't feel real until now. Every time we think of a place, we pull it up on Google Maps and mark it as a favorite. By the time we're done with dinner, the map of the U.S. looks like a Christmas tree with the stars of all the places we've saved.

The next week is a blur. Inspectors seem to be coming through the house every other day and despite the fact that we have a buyer who's pre-approved, John continues to hold open houses on the weekends and show the house during the week. Kait and I have been working from home almost every day and have enjoyed watching John give tours of the house.

The first time John gave a tour of the house while we were home, I was sitting in the front of the motorhome and looked up to see a family staring back at me from the kitchen. We all waved at each other and then I went back to work. Whenever John shows the house now, we make sure to close the blinds and pretend we're not inside.

Friday, August 7th, 2015

As part of my Friday routine, I check my bank account to make sure my paycheck came through. Today, I notice a second, much larger amount. There's no description of what this money is for, but I can see it's from my company. Logging into my company portal, I check my account and notice the extra payment is my retention bonus.

"Babe!" I say yanking the bathroom door open scaring Kait half to death.

"You scared me! I'm trying to take a shower."

"My bonus came through this morning!"

"Wait, what? I thought that it would take 30 days to go through. It's only been a week."

"That's what they told us, but apparently it didn't take that long."

"So does this mean you're going to put in your notice next week?"

"No, I want to wait until we know that we're going to close on the house. I'm worried that if the sale doesn't go through it might take a few more months before we can leave. John was telling me that if we aren't able to sell now, the rules for escrow recently changed and we'll have to do a 60-day escrow rather than the standard 30. That means at least another two months if this sale falls through."

"Good point. Well, like I said, I don't think we have anything to worry about."

The house inspection reports are starting to come through, but we're still waiting for the final overall report. According to the buyer's agent, there are a number of issues they want taken care of. Most of these are things I can deal with, however the most concerning report is the one from the termite inspector.

"So what do we do about the termite report?" I ask John over the phone.

"Nothing right now. It seems they found traces of termites under and around the house. The report suggests that we'll have to tent the house in order to fix the problem and the buyers are asking us to do the work prior to closing. I want to bring in another company that I've worked with for a second opinion. There are other solutions and I think it was a bit premature to suggest that we have to tent the house. They also want to bring in an electrician to look at the breaker box. According to the report, the panel is a safety concern because of the age and type of breakers it uses."

"I don't think we have the time before closing to get this work done," I tell John. "We'd rather give them a credit and they can get everything taken care of."

"I agree, but this is all part of the dance we have to do with the buyers. Let me get on the phone with the other agent and see what we can work out."

"Thanks. By the way, can you also ask if they are going to buy the appliances? I'm going to need some time to sell them if they aren't interested."

The more we seem to dance with the buyers, the more it seems like they want to pull out of the deal. We've spent almost a week haggling over details. The termite issue has been the biggest pain. The second report wasn't nearly as dire as the first, but the buyers don't want to budge. We also disagree on the cost to fix the electrical issues their inspector found. The buyers are asking for an exorbitant amount in credits so we counter again with an amount we're willing to give them and stipulate that this offer is final. Kait and I are both getting stressed over this whole ordeal. Every day there seems to be another issue or something to haggle over. I don't know if we have the patience to go through this process again if the deal falls through. It would also mean at least another two months of work. That doesn't sound like much, but it's like telling a kid on Christmas they're going to have to wait a few weeks to open their presents. Or in Kait's case, asking her to make a batch of Chinese dumplings then telling her she has to wait a week before eating them.

If the stress at home wasn't enough, the climate at work has changed quite a bit since the merger. Teams from the new company are auditing our work and the audits mean more reports, meetings and long hours at the office. It's tough to watch them break down many of the projects I've helped build over the years, but it's their company now and they can do what they want. With everything going on, it feels like our lives are in turmoil. There are a lot of moving parts that need to come together in order for us to leave and start to live the life we've been planning. It's a giant puzzle with a few pieces left, but the pieces are nowhere to be found.

The new company is a behemoth, and they're adding layer upon layer of new procedures and methods that have to be followed. One bright spot is that they've shut down my ability to get work emails on my personal phone. Everyone at the company who uses their phone to get email is required to install this security app. I refused to install the app so my mobile email account was terminated. The heads of my department have been hounding me to put in a requisition to get a company phone, but at this stage what's the point? I've been toying with the idea of putting in my notice just so I don't have to play this game anymore. Then I can focus on helping them transition my role to someone else.

Tuesday, August 18th, 2015

I'm rushing to get out of the motorhome this morning because I have an in-person meeting to attend. Tossing my laptop bag in the back seat, I jump in the Jeep and hit play on the latest episode of The Survival Podcast, "Episode 1626, Do it Now." Backing out of the drive way I feel one of the tires go over a large bump. Getting out I see what I ran over and panic. "My morning is ruined and I don't have time to fix this," I think to myself. In my haste, I left my steel coffee tumbler sitting on the rear bumper of the Jeep and it must have fallen as I was backing out. Picking it up, I notice that some of the paint has been scratched off and there is a sizable dent in the side, but all is good in the world because very little of the coffee spilled. Don't know what I would have done with out my morning cup of coffee.

By the time I'm on the parking lot that is the 405 Freeway, the podcast is in full swing and Jack is telling a story about a listener who emailed him. The listener had a friend who was in his mid-40's and suddenly passed away from a brain aneurysm. The friend had planned on doing all these things later in life but died before he was able to do any of them. After Jack is finished with the story and how it relates to his show for the day, he says, "You don't know when your time is up." He follows that up a minute later with, "the time is NOW to start living life under your own terms with a plan." I don't need any other explanation. Turning off the podcast, I call Kait on the Jeep's Bluetooth.

"Hey hon, what's up?"

"I'm putting in my notice today. I was listening to my podcast and Jack said a few things about how unsure life can be. It gave me a kick in the ass and I'm done postponing our

plans. If the house doesn't sell, I'm sure we can work something out with John to sell it while we're on the road or
maybe rent it. Regardless, I'm taking the next step."

"I'm so excited for you. I know this has been hanging
over your head and you've been looking forward to this day
for a long time. If you're going to put in your notice, I'm also
going to put in mine. I'll have to wait until my boss is back in
the office tomorrow. Have a great day and call me after you
do it. I want all the details."

"Are you sure you're good with me doing this?"

"Absolutely. You're 100% right. We've delayed long
enough and if the buyer backs out, we have other options."

As excited as I am, I feel regret for not having done this
sooner. I took the easy and comfortable route, choosing to
play it safe rather than take a risk, but I can't change the past.
I can only affect what happens next and I've taken the steps I
need to make those changes in my life.

My morning meetings fly by with talk about projects
kicking off in 2016. I can barely muster a feigned interest
because I'll be long gone by then. Tim, the head of my department and the one who initially offered me the retention
bonus, calls into the last teleconference meeting from New
York. Right before the meeting ends, I ask Tim if he can hold
on for a few minutes. Once everyone has dropped off the
call, I pick up the receiver.

"Sorry to keep you Tim, but there is something I need to
discuss with you."

"This can't be good, what's up?"

"I'm putting in my notice today. I wanted to let you
know before I called Steve."

There is a minute of silence on the phone before Tim responds. "Where are you going?"

"Well, that's the interesting part. My wife and I bought a motorhome and we're in the process of selling our house. Once it's sold, we're going to hit the road for a year to travel the country and take some time off."

"That sounds incredible and something I wish I could do, but speaking as your friend, are you sure this is what you want to do? There is talk of a promotion for you, and you're being put onto projects that the new company is prioritizing. If you hang on for at least another six months, the second half of your retention bonus will be paid out. You'll be giving up a lot by leaving right now."

"I've thought extensively about that, but now is the time. There will always be some other hook to keep me from leaving and I've realized that this is not something I want to postpone any longer. When my dad passed away, he told me to take risks in life and that's exactly what I'm doing. My wife and I have been planning this for a while and we're ready to get on the road."

"Like I said, this is something I wish I could do, but I wanted to make sure you understood what you're leaving. I wish you the best of luck and am happy for the two of you, I'm sorry to do this but I'm late for my next meeting and need to run. Talk soon."

Since I still have the room to myself, I pick up the phone again and call Steve who is my direct boss based in New York.

"Hey Steve, this is Joe. Do you have a few minutes?"

"Hey Joe, you caught me at the perfect time. I've got another meeting in twenty minutes and I'm booked the rest of the day. What's on your mind?"

"Well Steve, I'm calling to tell you I'm putting in my notice."

Steve seems much more taken aback than Tim and I explain what Kait and I will be doing for the next year.

"This is normally the point in the conversation when I would ask what I can do to keep you," Steve says. "However, I don't think there is anything I could offer you that would be better than what you have planned, is there?"

"No Steve, this is something we've planned for the last year. We're ready to move on with this next chapter in our lives. I appreciate the offer however and have enjoyed working with you and the team."

"You've been a great asset and I'm sorry to be losing you. Have you given any thought to when your last day will be?"

"I have. My wife and I still have a few things to take care of before we leave and I want to make my last day Friday, September 4th."

"Three weeks. That will be good, we have a lot we'll need to transition and make sure we're up to speed on all your projects. I'm sorry to see you go, but wish you and your wife the best of luck. If you decide that you want to come back after a year, give me a call."

This was a huge hurdle for me to get over. There were times during the last year I seriously considered staying and would have jumped at an offer from Steve for a promotion or a raise, but like I told him, I'm ready to take that next step in our lives. It's time to take risks.

With my meetings finished and nothing else left for the day, I head home early to beat the traffic.

26. ALWAYS BE CLOSING

Friday, August 21st, 2015

Work has become even busier. Once word got around that I was leaving, all the departments I work with asked to meet so we could work out transition plans. One of the biggest projects I have been working on started in 2009. I've been on it since day one and many people are afraid that when I leave, a huge repository of knowledge about the project will leave with me. In some ways it feels great to be needed, but it's also taxing. I have two weeks to go until my last day and it can't come soon enough.

As I am walking to my next meeting my cell phone rings.

"Hello?"

"Joe, it's John."

Over the last few weeks, John has become much more serious on the phone. I know Kait and I are both stressed about the house and he probably is too. The prospect of the sale falling through is wearing on all of us.

"Hey John, what's going on?"

"I have some good news. The buyers have accepted all of our terms regarding the credits in lieu of performing the repairs. I just got off the phone with escrow and the buyer's agent. We're pushing to have everything done by next Thursday or Friday. There will be a lot of movement in the next week so be ready for a flood of emails with documents that need your signatures."

"That's a huge relief. We were beginning to wonder if the sale was going to fall through. Hey, did they mention anything about the appliances? I need to know soon otherwise I'm going to sell them."

"I asked the buyer's agent again and she told me that they are going to stop by the house on Monday to look at them and give us a response. I'd suggest pulling out any manuals you have for the appliances and leaving them out. That usually makes people feel better about buying something used."

"I'll take care of that tonight. So I guess we need to plan to be out of there by Friday then."

"Actually, I'd suggest trying to be out by Thursday as the buyers will most likely take possession Friday morning."

"Alright, will do. I'm sure we'll be talking a lot over the next week. Thanks John."

Saturday morning, Kait and I open the garage door and look across the sea of stuff that is still in there. The dent I made a few weeks ago is hardly noticeable and I feel like we've somehow moved more stuff in. The new bumper for the Jeep finally arrived and that's sitting in the garage waiting for installation. We have other things that are staged in the garage, waiting for us to move them into the motorhome.

"Here's what I suggest we do," I tell Kait. "Let's get the bumper installed. That will free up some room. Then we can focus on moving everything that needs to go into the motorhome. We can tackle everything else later."

"I like your plan. Do you need my help to install the bumper?"

"I think I will. Let me grab my tools and we can get started."

As much as I will miss having a garage, I have to admit that having everything I need in the bays of the motorhome is making life easy. No more hunting down tools or having to figure out which one of twenty screw drivers I want to use. I can see why the minimalist lifestyle has taken hold. My life is no longer about the accumulation of things I don't need, but rather it is focused on getting rid of all but the essential things that are well-made and can do what I need to get done.

It doesn't take long to get the bumper on the Jeep with Kait's help. I'm excited about how it's changed the look of the Wrangler to be manlier now. The stock bumper is in great shape so I take a few photos to see if I can sell it online. Until then, it will have to sit in the garage. So much for making room.

"Before we move stuff into the motorhome, I want to organize the bays," Kait says. "You just kind of threw stuff in there and I want to straighten them out before we put anything else in. Why don't you work on going through everything else in the garage that we can sell, giveaway or throw out."

I have shelves around the whole interior perimeter of the garage and they are as full as the rest of the garage. Over the course of the next hour I fill up the two garbage cans and move on to filling up plastic bags with more stuff to throw away. There are still some old tools and items that I don't want to get rid of so I put them aside. By the time I've cleared the shelves, it's after 6 p.m. and I haven't even made it to the piles on the floor. Kait finished organizing the bays and is loading a few smaller items in. They're getting full, and I doubt we'll be able to fit much more in them which means I need to reevaluate most of what I have set aside.

"Let's call it a night," I tell Kait. "I'm beat and we can pick it up again tomorrow. Why don't you get cleaned up and I'll pick up something for dinner."

"Sounds good to me. I've been craving Thai food from the place down the street. Get the spicy noodle dish I like."

"Okay, I'll call it in on my way there. Be back in a bit."

The rest of the weekend is spent trying to clean out the garage. Our garbage cans are full and our neighbor no longer has the huge dumpster.

"It's a good thing our garbage is getting picked up on Wednesday," Kait says.

"I still don't know where we are going to fit everything. What do you think about boxing up the items we want to keep but don't have room for and leaving them at my mom's house?"

"What all do we have to store there?"

"Our pictures and memorabilia like your wedding dress. We have a few pairs of shoes, clothes, tools and some of your kitchen equipment. I want to keep a few of these things in case we move back into a house again. No point in throwing it out if we can find some room for it at my mom's."

"All right, but I don't want to fill up her garage with stuff. We should get rid of as much as possible."

Monday, August 24th, 2015

The emails from John and the escrow company have started flooding our inbox. One after another with paperwork to review, sign and send back. I'm getting a lot of the same documents to sign and I've been asked to sign some that I have already taken care of. I step into an empty conference room and give Kait a call.

"Hey honey, I'm pretty busy what up?" She asks.

"Have you seen all the emails about the house?"

"I have, but haven't we already signed a lot of those?"

"We have. With all of the back and forth, I'm getting concerned that something will slip through the cracks. I asked John to come over this evening so we can review the paperwork and make sure we're not missing anything."

"That's a great idea."

That evening, John shows up with his briefcase and we all sit down at the folding table. As we go through each document, John checks to make sure we've signed it. We find out there is one document that still needs our signatures. Otherwise, it looks like everything is in order.

"One last thing," John asks. "Do you want the proceeds from the sale wired to an account or would you prefer a check?"

"Check please," Kait replies. "I don't want to pay the fee to wire the funds when I can walk the check down to the bank and deposit it myself."

"Okay we can do that. I finally heard back from the buyer's agent, they don't want your appliances. In my opinion, they were stringing you along until the last moment hoping you'd be too busy moving out and would just leave them."

I'm normally pretty calm about things, but I don't like to be strung along. Shaking my head I look up at John and say, "I will give those things away if I have to. There is no way I am leaving them anything."

"I completely understand and gave the agent a piece of my mind. Well, unless escrow needs anything else, the next time we meet I will have your check. When you guys do vacate the house tomorrow, leave the keys on the sink and lock the doors behind you. I will give them my spare."

After John leaves, I decide to take a break from clearing out the garage and snap some photos of the appliances to list on Craigslist. I'm a very honest person with people and when someone tries to get one over on me by doing something like this, I am bound and determined not to let them get away with it. In about fifteen minutes, I have responses from multiple people eager to check out the appliances. I guess when you are selling high end appliances for a small fraction of the cost, people jump right on it.

Less than an hour after the first ad went up, a family arrives to buy the washer and dryer. I never disconnected anything because I figured they would stay in the house so I grab my tools to undo the water and gas lines. Once I'm done, a few of the guys haul the appliances out just as a woman and her son walk up the driveway to see the refrigerator. They have a dolly in tow so I know they mean business. After a quick examination and a handshake, the woman hands me two hundred dollar bills, and her son straps the fridge to the dolly.

"So you're selling the house?" She asks.

"Yep, anything you see here that isn't bolted down is for sale."

"How much do you want for this clock?" She asks pointing to a nice clock we have hanging in the kitchen.

"$5" I say and she pulls a fiver from her pocket and hands it to me.

"You have a very nice house. What about those two planters outside?"

"Since you've been so nice, they're yours if your son can grab them. They are solid concrete."

True to my word, everything she points out that we don't have to contractually leave in the house I sell for pennies on the dollar or give to her for free. By the time she and her son leave, the bed of their pickup is overflowing and the house is picked clean. "I wonder what they'll think when they show up Friday morning and all the appliances are gone," I say to myself, standing in the empty kitchen with a huge smile on my face.

Back in the garage, Kait has finished packing everything we're going to store at my mother's house.

"Why don't I take over a load tonight and we can bring the rest tomorrow," I tell her. "I'm also going to bring the boys over so my mom can watch them while we're busy trying to get everything done here."

"Sounds good. All of these boxes are ready to go. Were you able to sell everything?"

"Everything that wasn't bolted down."

"Good job, honey."

I've been going over to my mother's the last two nights to clean out her garage so we have room to store our boxes. When I arrive, she has a plate of leftovers heating in the microwave for me and a pot of fresh coffee. I'm starving so the food is a welcome distraction, and I'll never turn down a fresh cup of coffee. After I'm done eating, it takes about an hour to get everything put away. I don't get home until after 11 p.m. and Kait is sound asleep. We both have to be in the office every day this week and we've been up past midnight trying to get everything moved out of the garage. Thankfully the motorhome is loaded and ready to go, but there are still odds and ends we're finding that we want to bring with us.

Thursday after work, I drive the motorhome over to my mother's house. Kait is going to meet me there after work so she can drive me back and we can pack up the last remaining items. My mother offered to let us set up camp in front of her house and have free use of the guest bedroom, if we need it. Our parents are extremely generous people who have offered us a place to stay if we ever need it. As we get ready to leave behind everything we know, realizing we have places to stay and people who are willing to help if we need it, is a huge reassurance for us. Embarking on our upcoming adventure would be more difficult if we didn't have the support of our families.

Our friends on the other hand have been a mixed bag. Many of them are supportive and have told us they want to visit us on the road. Other's think we're crazy for wanting to do this and don't think we'll last more than a few months. Then we have friends and some extended family who believe that we're making a bad decision to leave "secure" jobs, retirement benefits and health care to live on the open road. I've seen how "secure" some jobs could be every time we've had lay-offs at the company.

The sun is just starting to go down when I get the motorhome on the road. It's rush hour and heading west, the sun is directly in my eyes. I remember that the front shade can be used as a sun shield when driving. Reaching over, I press the button to lower the shade and hold it until it's where I want it to be. It doesn't stop. I try hitting the "up" button but the shade continues all the way down. It's a black out shade and my entire view of the road is blocked at this point. There isn't anywhere to pull over so I come to a stop in the middle of the road and retract the front shade enough so that I can see out of the window again.

By the time I make it to my mom's house, Kait is there and helps me park along the curb without hitting the large tree in front of the house. With the motorhome settled, we drive back to the house in Kait's Honda so we can finish cleaning out the garage.

"Should we try and donate some of this stuff?" Kait asks looking at everything we have left.

"Let's put any of the donation items aside for now. There is still a lot we need to load into the cars to store at my mom's house. I don't know how much room we'll have left. At least the garbage cans were emptied yesterday."

Kait gathers all the items for donation while I work on putting everything else away. In less than an hour, the garbage cans are full again and I begin packing our cars with everything we want to store. Luckily we have some room left for the donation items. What we can't fit into the cars gets shoved into the garbage cans. Every time I think they are full, I manage to squeeze in one more thing. By 10:30 p.m., the garage is cleared out, and embracing each other, we say good-bye to our first house.

"We had some great times here. I'm going to miss this place," I tell Kait.

"I'm not going to miss it. We're going to be living on the road in a few weeks, how exciting is that?"

"You know how sentimental I am with things like this. I have a much harder time letting go than you do."

"Trust me, when we're making our way through the Rockies, the last thing you'll be thinking about is this house. Now go put the keys on the sink and let's get back to our home on wheels."

Friday, August 28th, 2015

One of the most hectic weeks of my life is finally over. According to the email I received this morning, all the paperwork is done and we closed on the house. John is going to hand deliver our check tonight. As Kait predicted, everything is falling right into place. There are still a few things left on our to do list, but after next week, we'll be done with work and almost ready to hit the road.

27. LAST DAY

Tuesday, September 1st, 2015

Yesterday, Kait left for a three-day business trip. It's our last week at work and we're ready to move on to the next chapter of our lives. Since we left the comforts of our driveway last week, we've been street camping in front of my mother's house. The plan is to stay here until we're ready to take off. I grew up in this house and know many of the neighbors that still live on the street. So far, they don't seem to care that our motorhome is parked here.

My mother has always wanted to be close to us and I think this is as close as we can get without living in the same house. She's thrilled to have us and I'm happy to be able to spend time with her before we drive off into the proverbial sunset. It's a strange experience because we have dinner with my mom, use her guest bathroom and then sleep in the motorhome. She did offer us the guest bedroom, but we graciously declined. There's nothing like being able to sleep in our own bed each night. That's the one thing I love about traveling in an motorhome, I get to have my own bed and pillow everywhere I go.

The downside of camping on the street is that we can only put the bedroom slide out. Since it's on the curbside of the motorhome, it's not blocking anything. If we put the driver's side slide out, we'd be blocking a portion of the road and run the risk of someone hitting it. The last thing we need is for the trash truck to rip the slide off as it drives by. Although the motorhome is manageable with the big slide in, it does feel cramped. Having my mom's house right outside has been a nice escape when I start to feel a bit claustrophobic. The boys love hanging out in the house because they have a huge yard to run around in plus my mother loves to spoil them with treats and love.

"Hey honey, I've got great news!" Kait says over the phone. "I was able to find a flight home tonight rather than getting in tomorrow morning. I'll be back around midnight and I can't wait to see you and the boys."

"That is great news. I'll wait up for you and can't wait to see you tonight."

The boys and I are watching TV in the motorhome when we hear Kait's car pull up. Despite the time, the boys are up and dancing around in excitement while I head out to help Kait with her bags. As Kait steps inside, she stops for a moment, says hello to the boys, puts her purse down and goes into the bedroom.

"What's wrong?" I ask.

"Nothing, I'm fine."

Now I know that something is wrong. That's the "there's something wrong and I'm either upset with you or I don't feel like talking about it," response. I decide to press anyway.

"Look, I know something is wrong," I say sitting down on the bed next to her. "Living in such tight quarters isn't going to work if you're not going to talk to me when there is a problem."

"You're right, I just didn't expect to feel this way,"

"What way?" I respond nervously.

"I don't know. When I got back I was so excited to see you and the boys, but when I walked in and saw the motorhome, I...well, it was too much to handle."

"I still don't get it, what do you mean it was too much to handle? The fact that we're living in a motorhome?"

"No, I wasn't prepared to come home to the motorhome all closed up. When I walked in, it didn't feel like I was coming home. It felt like I was coming back to a box that we're half living out of while spending the other half in your mom's house. It made me feel very unsettled. I think I'll be fine once we get on the road and this becomes our full time home. Sorry, with the stress of the last couple of days, this just put me over the edge and I'm feeling much better now that I got that out. Thank you for pushing me to talk about it."

"Of course. I know how you feel. It's strange for me too, I've just had a few more days than you to get accustomed to it."

Thursday, September 3rd, 2015

Some of my coworkers are throwing me a going away party after work. I don't want to worry about driving home, so I decide to drive Kait's car to work and leave it there overnight. She's going to pick me up at the office in the Jeep and drive us to the party then home.

Over the last few days, I've been wrapping things up with the various teams and saying my goodbyes. As excited as I am to be moving on, I'm starting to feel very emotional about leaving. Ten years is a long time to work at one company and I've made some great friends. I've been dreaming about the day I can walk away from this place and now that it's here, it's harder than I envisioned.

I've talked about myself being a slave to corporate America, but I've come to the realization that I willingly put the shackles on. I wasn't working to grow as a person and change the world. I was working to make money and buy more stuff. The more money I earned, the more I would spend. We bought a house, nice cars and things that would simply end up taking more space in the closet rather than adding value to our lives. Weekends were spent at the mall and going out to fancy dinners. Subsequently, weekdays were spent dreaming about what we would buy next.

The act of selling the house, getting rid of most of my possessions except for the ones I absolutely need, and no longer working for someone else for the foreseeable future has given me a freedom I've never felt before. There's no more room to collect things that aren't essential, especially with Kait's one-in-one-out rule. If I need to buy something, then something will have to go. The decision to trade material things for life experiences has already made a noticeable difference in my life.

As I walk through the office saying my goodbyes, everyone is excited for me. There is a bit of jealousy in the air as I can tell many of them wish they could let go and live free. We figured out a way to break away and live now, rather than wait until we're in our 60s to enjoy life. The one thing I hear the most from people at work is the same thing I heard when we had our party, "I wish I could do what you guys are doing." Everyone here willingly put on those same shackles. Most of them are resigned to spend the majority of their life working in hopes that one day they will have saved enough to retire and live the life that they've always wanted.

The problem, as Jack stated in his podcast a few weeks ago, is that we have no idea what tomorrow will bring. The only guarantee in life is death and no one knows if they'll live long enough to see retirement. Even if we do live to our 60s, will we be healthy enough to enjoy it? I've spoken to a lot of people lately, and they all wish they could live the life of their dreams, but sadly they all have one reason or another why they can't.

At the top of the list are children, debt, family, mortgages and the list goes on. There are young families living on the road full time with children and they're able to make it work. I want to tell them that they have to be willing to take a risk and even sacrifice things in order to get what they want. You may not be able to buy that new sports car, but instead of coming into the office every day, you can live your dream.

Most people aren't ready to act. I wasn't when Kait came up with the idea and dismissed her as crazy. It's not easy to go against social norms, but I'm hopeful that we can show people through example that it can be done. Whether it's traveling through Europe, driving around the U.S. in a motorhome or something else entirely, all that's required is the willingness to make the change. Take control of your life and take risks.

That evening, Kait and I are the first to arrive at the party. It's a popular bar by the beach that has a great selection of local beers. I order an IPA that is made right down the street as we grab a table and wait for everyone to arrive. There's nothing quite like a perfectly chilled draft beer on a warm day.

Once I'm about half way through the IPA, people start to trickle in. It's starting to feel more like a retirement party than one of those parties for someone moving on to a different company. My friends seem to be genuinely excited and look forward to hearing about our adventures. Most still think we're crazy and after everyone's had a few beers, I hear more than one time that I "have huge balls for doing something like this." It's a great evening and I realize that this will be the last time I see most of these people. We plan to be on the road for a year and have no idea where we'll end up, but we do know it will not be back in Los Angeles or California for that matter.

As we talk about our initial travel plans, everyone shares their suggestions on places to visit across the country. Some have even said they want to meet up with us for a long week end when we make it to certain parts of the country. I'm looking forward to that and wonder how many people will actually make the trek to visit us while we're on the road. The party wraps up around 10 p.m. and at this time, the traffic is actually manageable on the freeways.

It's Friday morning, our last day at work. Kait and I decide to drive together in the Jeep. Since I left the Honda at work and Kait drove us home last night, she's going to drop me off and then head to work. They're throwing a going away lunch for her and she invited me to join. Once I finish up a few things and have my exit interview, I'll drive over and meet her for lunch.

"I've been thinking that we should start some kind of daily video journal about what we're doing," I tell Kait as we get on the freeway. "It might be fun to show people what we're doing plus we might be able to make some money through YouTube."

"You mean like a VLOG?"

"Exactly. Maybe a two to three minute video each day to tell people what we're up to. We can share our experiences and maybe we'll help other people realize their dream to live the life they want."

"I think that's a great idea honey," Kait says as she reaches into her purse pulling out her phone. She holds it up and points it at me.

"What are you doing?"

"This is going to be the first VLOG," Kait says and starts talking to the camera. "Joe and I are driving to our last day of work together..."

It feels very strange to have a camera pointed at me while I'm trying to drink my morning coffee and drive. Plus I've never been good at coming up with something on the fly. "I'm not sure I can do this on a regular basis."

"It takes practice and you're not going to be very good right away. We're just going to have to keep at it."

Once we get to my office, I kiss Kait goodbye and promise to see her in a few hours for lunch. Walking into the building, I'm reminded of my first day and how much things have changed. I never thought I would be here for so long but here I am, one month after my 10-year anniversary, walking into the office for the last time.

Last week Steve called to tell me that he was sending me my 10-year anniversary plaque along with a catalogue to pick out a gift from the company. "Better make sure you put the order in now, otherwise I don't know if you'll ever get it," he said and we both had a good laugh.

My exit interview goes by quickly since I'm not going to another company. Typically, HR asks people why they're leaving, what it is about the company they're going to that drew them in, that sort of thing. The person from HR realizes that I don't have much to share in that regard and wishes me well on my travels. As I am leaving I get the, "I wish I could do that" line I've become so accustomed to hearing.

I've already said my goodbyes so when I get back to my desk, I grab a few things to take home. I won't be walking out of the office with the typical big brown box. Most of what I have went to my coworkers or into the trash. There is no room in the motorhome for more stuff aside from some photos and little knick-knacks that I decided to hold on to. Jenny and I say our goodbyes and promise to stay in touch. With a final wave, I walk into the elevator and out of the office for the last time.

Traffic is worse than I expected and I'm about thirty minutes late for Kait's lunch, but as I walk in, I see I haven't missed much. Appetizers are just starting to arrive and I'm starving. There seems to be a much more somber attitude at her lunch compared to my party last night. Since they have such a small team, with Kait leaving, their workloads are going to increase quite a bit. Despite that, they are all very excited for us and Kait seems happier than she has in a long time. I can tell she's come to the same realization I have about leaving our jobs.

"Well honey, are you ready to get going?" Kait asks as I finish my sixth cup of coffee.

"I'm ready."

Standing up, I say goodbye to everyone at the table and follow Kait out of the restaurant. Stepping into the sun, we both feel reborn. This moment is the start of our new lives.

28. WARRANTY WOES

Kait and I drive separately as we make our way to my mother's house after her farewell lunch. Once we arrive, I spot a large package on her doorstep. The tow bar I ordered has been on back order and, unless my mother ordered something sizable, this should be it. Examining the label, I see my hunch is correct. It's our ReadyBrute Elite tow bar. I'm relieved that I had the foresight to ship it here rather than to our old house because who knows what the new owners would have done with a package this size on their doorstep. With the motorhome going in for warranty work on Monday, I'll need to complete the installation this weekend.

Saturday afternoon, I have the Jeep pulled into my mother's garage with parts and tools scattered all over the place. My method of organization is to make as big of a mess as possible. Despite the mess, when I am under the Jeep, I can reach over and grab any tool I need without looking. This drives Kait nuts, but it works for me. After about four hours of work, the sun is going down and I still have a lot left to do. Time to call it quits for the day and pick it back up tomorrow. I'm happy with the progress and ready for a hot cup of coffee.

I'm up early Sunday and get back to work on the Jeep. By lunch time, I am finished installing all of the wiring and cables for the brake system.

"How's it going out there?" Kait asks as I come in to grab a glass of water and something to munch on.

"Pretty good, I think I'm ready to get it hooked up to the motorhome and finish the installation. After lunch, I'll need your help to get things lined up and adjusted correctly."

"I have a couple things to finish up in here and then I'll be out to help."

With Kait's help, it doesn't take long to finish the installation and we're ready for a test-drive. The main concern is to make sure that the cable running from the tow bar to the Jeep's brake pedal isn't too tight or too loose.

"Why don't I drive down the street and hit the brakes while you walk alongside to see if the brakes are being activated?"

"I'm ready."

Our first test goes well. As I hit the brakes on the motorhome, I see Kait giving me a thumbs up in the mirror.

"Looks like everything is working well," she says.

"Great. Now I want to test it at a normal driving speed."

"I can climb in the Jeep and watch the pedal as you're driving down the road," Kait suggests.

"Great idea. Hop in and I'll drive us around the neighborhood."

"Okay, let me grab our walkie-talkies so I can talk to you from the Jeep."

We bought a set of walkie-talkies so we could communicate when I am trying to back into a tight spot or if Kait needs to drive the Jeep separately. "I'm ready. Over," Kait says on the radio. I pull away from the curb and start driving around the neighborhood. There is an empty street that's long enough to get some speed and test the system. Turning onto the street, I gun the motorhome and get it up to 40 mph, then brake hard.

"The brake pedal looks like it's moving just fine. How does the motorhome feel? Over."

"I don't notice the extra weight from the Jeep. I'm going to head down another street and try it again. Over."

Looking at the rear camera, I see Kait giving me the thumbs up from inside the Jeep.

"It looks like everything is working well," Kait says once we're back in front of my mother's house. "I think it's adjusted perfectly."

"That's good to hear because I am worn out and ready to stop messing with this thing. The real test will be tomorrow when we take the motorhome to the shop and tow the Jeep behind it," I tell Kait.

The dealer we bought the motorhome from suggested we take it to a local RV repair shop that specializes in Newmars. They have the initial list of warranty items to be addressed, but I was told to keep adding to the list as more things come up. The list has continued to grow the more we've used the motorhome.

Before we leave, we hook up the Jeep to the tow bar. Kait seems to be much better at lining the Jeep up with the motorhome and attaching the tow bar, so we agree that it's her job going forward. We make it to the repair shop before 9 a.m. and I'm hoping that if we can be one of the first RVs in the shop that day, we can have it back tonight or tomorrow at the latest.

"It's amazing how well the Jeep towed behind the motorhome," I say to Kait. "I had no problems switching lanes and didn't even know it was there. Plus, I like being able to keep an eye on it with the rear view camera."

"I can't wait for my turn to tow the Jeep."

"Well, if we pick up the motorhome during the day, you can drive us home. I'm just hoping we get it back tonight."

We walk into the main office and ring the bell at the service counter. A minute later, a woman is there to greet us.

"Hi, how can I help you?" She asks.

"We're here to get some warranty work done," I respond.

"Uh, sorry we don't do warranty work here, you'll need to go somewhere else."

I'm speechless for a moment. This was the shop that our dealer suggested. How could they not do warranty work? I even told them over the phone when I made the appointment that I was bringing the motorhome in for warranty work. This was the last thing on our list to get done and we are planning on taking off once we get it back. If they can't take us, then I'm sure other shops will have a month or two wait list as well. "Calm down," I tell myself. "Don't panic."

"When I called to make the appointment, I specifically said it was for warranty work. No one said that would be a problem."

"You would have been speaking to me. What's your name? Let me look up your appointment."

"Joe Russo."

"Russo, Russo, Russo," she repeats looking at her computer.

"Ah here it is. No, you're fine. You have a Newmar."

A wave of relief rolls over me. "Thank you. You had me scared there for a moment."

"Sorry about that. Newmar is the only company that we work with for warranty repairs. We used to do warranty work for a few other brands, but it took them so long to approve the work and send reimbursements that we decided to drop everyone except for Newmar. Let me get Jimmy, he's going to be your tech and will go through your list with you."

A few minutes later Jimmy meets us at the motorhome. I have a handwritten list of all the issues we've found and Jimmy walks through the motorhome inspecting each issue to make sure we're on the same page about what needs to be done.

"These should all be pretty easy to take care of. I'm going to have to take a few pictures for approval and have some parts ordered. Otherwise, I should be able to knock everything out in a few days to a week depending on how quickly Newmar gets back to me."

"When will you know how long it will take?" Kait asks.

"I should know by tomorrow. I'm going to get everything submitted to Newmar today for approval and I should hear back early tomorrow. They may call you if they have any additional questions and I'll give you a call once I know more."

Walking back to the Jeep Kait looks over and says, "I didn't think it could take a week. I thought the longest it might take would be a day or two. I'm so accustomed to taking my car into the shop and getting it back later that day. Having to leave the motorhome for a week didn't even cross my mind."

"I've heard stories of some people having to leave their RV for months while work is being done. I don't even want to think about something like that happening once we're on the road."

"I guess we'll have to live out of your mom's house for a few days. Wait, we should go in and grab our stuff. Clothes, toiletries and anything that's in the fridge that might go bad."

"Great idea, I didn't even think about that."

After we grab all of our stuff for the next week, we head back to my mom's house. It feels very strange to leave our "house" with someone else. Over the next few days, we don't hear from Jimmy and finally give him a call to see what's going on. He got approval for everything and the parts came in today so he should be done with the motorhome by Friday.

"I was hoping to leave this week, but why don't we plan to pick it up on Saturday and take off early Sunday morning?" Kait asks.

"I'm good with that. It will be nice to get our home back." That's one huge difference between living in a motorhome versus living in a sticks and bricks house. When we had work done on the house, we didn't have to take it anywhere and leave it with someone. They come to us and fix the problem. Another thing we have to adjust to with our new life style.

29. BALL OF FLAMES

Sunday, September 13th, 2015

We picked up the motorhome from the shop yesterday morning. Jimmy did a much better job than we anticipated. Many of the items he fixed looked better than when we bought the motorhome. Earlier in the week, we sold Kait's Honda. She bought it brand new after getting her first job out of college, right before meeting me. That was the one thing she had a difficult time letting go. With the Jeep ready to be flat towed and the motorhome packed, we're over the final hurdles. All that needs to be done this morning is to say our goodbyes, connect the Jeep and embrace the journey of our new life on the road. A life of freedom, where we have full control.

The last few months have been some of the most stressful for us. Right now, that stress is gone, replaced with excitement and uncertainty. We have no idea what lies ahead for us, but we can't wait to find out. As we've been getting closer to this day, I've increasingly wondered whether a year on the road would be enough. We only planned for a year, but I feel as though we're leaving our old lives behind for good. We got rid of nearly everything that wasn't essential. Excess clothes, furniture, appliances, keepsakes, tools, vehicles, the house...it's all gone. There is an air of finality to that, like we subconsciously decided that we'd never be going back to that kind of life. I don't know what will happen in a year when the money runs out. I can almost say for certain that we won't be back in a house, restarting the life we've left behind.

The modern definition of success tells us that we have to constantly acquire the latest and greatest things. We've become a throw away society. Rather than buying a pair of pants to last the next few years, we buy them for a night on the town, never to be worn again. That's who we were, not who we've become. Over the past year, we've redefined "success" to mean happy, healthy and living the life that we want and on our own terms. Not what others dictate.

My mother is going out for the day and gives us a teary goodbye. She wishes us luck and a safe journey before walking out the door. She doesn't think she can stand to watch us drive away so she's headed to the beach. We feed the boys and ourselves, head back into the garage to make sure we have everything we need. I get the bicycles loaded onto the Jeep and throw a couple more tools in as well.

Our first stop is going to be a Harvest Hosts vineyard in Central California. After seeing how much our friends enjoyed the program, we decided to join and are excited to try it out for ourselves. From there, we'll figure out where to go and what to do next. We've decided not to plan too far ahead and to let the wind take us where it might. As much as we'd love to see the whole country, we know that won't be possible in one year.

With everything loaded, we get the boys into the motorhome and pull the Jeep around to attach it. After we run through our checklist, we are ready for the open road. Putting the motorhome in drive, my heart is racing. So much has been building up to this very moment.

"You know," I say looking over at Kait as I take my foot off the brake and we start to roll forward, "we did it. So many people said we wouldn't get here, but we actually did it. Regardless of what happens now, no one can take that away from us, even if we go up in a ball of flames, at least we did it."

Kait's smile goes from ear to ear. "This thing better not go up in flames, otherwise I want a refund!"

We pull onto the 101 Freeway and head north to our first destination on this year long journey to freedom.

AFTERWORD

Well, that's it for this book but the story isn't over. We only planned to do this for a year but after that first month, we agreed that we could never go back to the way things were. The second book in this series, *Tales From the Open Road: The Adventures and Misadventures of RV Living* picks up right where this book leaves off, our first day on the road.

The idea to write this book started because we are always asked why we decided to live this life. The next question, in rapid succession, is always how are we able to manage it. We'd give people the quick synopsis and, in turn, they'd say, "you should write a book." I thought it was a great idea. The more I thought about it, I realized I could not only tell our story but also provide a resource for people looking to make a change in their lives. I hope that in some way, I've inspired you to live the life you want if you're not doing so already.

If you enjoyed this book, the best thing you can do is to leave a review. This helps in so many ways because the more reviews a book has, the more discoverable it becomes.

To learn more about our adventure and to connect with us:
Website: weretherussos.com
YouTube: youtube.com/weretherussos
Facebook: facebook.com/weretherussos
To find out more about some of the products we use and mention in the book, head over to our store: weretherussos.com/our-store

Thank you!
    Joe Russo
    We're the Russos

ACKNOWLEDGEMENTS

First, Kevin Tumlinson. When Kevin had us on the Word-slinger Podcast and learned I was trying to write a book, he took it upon himself to mentor me through the process. I tried writing this book several times and never got past the first page until I got on the phone with Kevin and read his book, *30-Day Author*. It took me a lot longer than 30 days, but I got it done with his help. He's also responsible for the great description and foreword.

A big thank you goes out to my family and friends who encouraged me to write this and had faith that I could get it done. I especially owe a huge debt of gratitude to my mother and father-in-law who helped edit this book. They went above and beyond.

Finally, I have to thank my amazing wife Kait. It was her crazy idea that started this whole "life on the road" adventure, but it was her support and strength that made it come to fruition. She helped me through many stressful times and I'm eternally grateful. She's also the one who kept copious notes, is responsible for taking most of the pictures I included in the book and much of the editing. She read through the book at least five times (that I counted) and I'm amazed at her attention to detail. Without her, I would probably still be sitting in a cubicle wondering what to do with my life.

Oh, I almost forgot, my good friend coffee. Together, we can do anything.